ANN FAHL

Dancing with THREAD

Your Guide to Free-Motion Quilting

C&T PUBLISHING

Text and Artwork copyright © 2010 by Ann Fahl

Artwork copyright © 2010 by C&T Publishing, Inc.

Publisher: Amy Marson

Creative Director: Gailen Runge

Acquisitions Editor: Susanne Woods

Editor: Lynn Koolish

Technical Editors: Teresa Stroin and Carolyn Aune

Copyeditor/Proofreader: Wordfirm Inc.

Cover/Book Designer: Kristy Zacharias

Production Coordinator: Kirstie L. Pettersen

Production Editor: Alice Mace Nakanishi

Illustrator: Lon Eric Craven

Photography by Christina Carty-Francis and Diane Pedersen of C&T Publishing, Inc., unless otherwise noted.

Published by C&T Publishing, Inc., P.O. Box 1456, Lafayette, CA 94549

Library of Congress Cataloging-in-Publication Data

Fahl, Ann, 1947–

Dancing with thread : your guide to free-motion quilting / Ann Fahl.

    p. cm.

ISBN 978-1-57120-661-9 (softcover)

1. Patchwork. 2. Machine quilting. I. Title.

TT835.F3173 2010

746.46--dc22

                    2009026630

Printed in China

Dedication

In 1978 I took my first quilting class, and today I am the author of two books on the subject. This has taken an enormous amount of dedication, love, and time over the years. It never could have happened without my husband, Bob. He has supported and encouraged me all this time, endured burned dinners, quilt and manuscript deadlines, and thread and fabric snippets throughout the house. Rarely did he complain. Thank you, Bob. I love you.

—*Ann*

Contents

Why Machine Quilt? 4

Why Free-Motion Quilting? 6

Gallery 7

Tools and Supplies 23
Everything you need to be a free-spirited quilter

Decorative Thread and Bobbins. 28
Keys to success with thread

Batting and Backing 34
Battings and backings make the difference

Choosing and Marking
Quilting Designs 37
How to choose a quilting design and mark it
on the top and borders

Preparation for Quilting 40
How to clean up the top, block the top, baste
the quilt, and block the finished quilt

Machine Quilting Basics 45
Holding the quilt, managing machine speed,
starting and stopping, manipulating the quilt under
the machine, eliminating drag, and taking breaks

The Four Stages of Quilting 48
Stabilizing seams, detailing blocks or designs, the
decorative quilting, and quilting borders and corners

More Thoughts on Quilting 52
Signing your quilt, quilting density, beads and
embellishments, and quilting checklist

Let the Dancing Begin 54
The Ballerina: BEGINNING QUILTING, 54
Practice basic designs

The Choreographer: INTERMEDIATE QUILTING, 56
Use combinations of quilting designs, color dances,
and variations

The Improvisational Dancer:
ADVANCED QUILTING, 58
Use your instincts and organize on paper and photos,
ideas for borders, and doodling

The Jazz Dancer: INTUITIVE QUILTING, 61
Follow your inner spirit using all your experience to
create spontaneous patterns directly on the quilt

Projects 63
BASIC INSTRUCTIONS AND QUILTING MOTIFS, 64
Seams, fusing stems, appliqué instructions, and
quilting designs

BEGINNER PROJECT:
Table Runner Sampler, 70
Get started with a simple table runner

EXPERIENCED BEGINNER PROJECT:
Dancing Coneflowers, 74
Practice quilting motifs in large blocks

EXPERIENCED BEGINNER PROJECT:
Dancing in the Wind, 79
Quilt using a background print

INTERMEDIATE PROJECT:
Square Dancing, 85
Practice on a fused surface of squares

EXPERIENCED PROJECT:
Line Dancing under the Stars, 89
Improvise around coneflowers and stars

Quilting Problem Solving 92

About the Author 95

Resources 95

Why Machine Quilt?

My first ten years as a quilter were filled with hand work. I loved the time I spent quilting each evening, after the children were in bed. These few hours were relaxing and gave me something to look forward to. The problem was that I had so many ideas for quilts, I couldn't possibly make them all in a lifetime, let alone get them all quilted! With small children at home the most I could possibly finish was two traditional bed quilts per year. This just wasn't enough.

Machine quilting has been a part of my quiltmaking since the 1980s. Because of a tight budget, I purchased a 70-year-old green Singer to begin my machine-quilting career, using only monofilament on top and bobbin. This opened a big door for me. Instead of spending four to six months hand quilting, I could finish a quilt in less than a week! Since I was in the early stages of my quilting career, this could make a huge difference in the number of quilts I could make to sell.

Even if you don't make quilts to sell, you feel a sense of accomplishment by both making and quilting a piece yourself. If you have a sewing machine that allows you to lower the feed dogs, and you have a darning foot, then you can machine quilt. Why send out your quilts? You are missing the most rewarding part of the quilt-making process.

I've had five new machines since my first old green one, and I've been free-motion quilting for many years. It's amazing how I continue to improve and find new solutions to challenges that come my way. You will find this will happen with you if you make free-motion quilting one of your priorities.

Not too long ago I was quilting on the edge of a new quilt and became exhilarated as I watched patterns take shape, creating highlights and shadows on the surface. This was the afternoon that the ideas started to come together for this book. As I was quilting, I realized that perhaps my childhood dream of wanting to be a ballerina with pink dancing slippers was coming true. I was dancing with thread on the quilt border with my sewing machine.

Yes, you have to practice free-motion quilting; but after you get the basic idea and become comfortable with the process, you will find that it can be relaxing and calming. With this book, I hope to help you refine your process, develop a personal style, and become a more free-spirited quilter. Put your old ideas and expectations away. Try something a little different.

There are many books on the market today that are filled with quilting motifs and patterns; this book is not. I suggest that you collect designs that interest you and put them in a notebook. This will provide you with your own convenient personalized collection of patterns that will help you begin to dance on your quilt, just as I have.

Since you are reading this book, you are ready to start this experience. This journey has a beginning and will continue as long as you quilt—there is no end! The more time you can dedicate to it, the more proficient you will become.

Come on, let me show you how to dance with thread on *your* quilt!

THREE TRILLIUM, *Ann Fahl © 2007, 38″ × 33″, wool batting*

Quilted leaves, loops, and flowers are all over surface.

Why Free-Motion Quilting?

Detail of **THREE TRILLIUM** *(quilt on page 5)*

Free-motion quilting is accomplished with the feed dogs down, allowing the quilter to easily move the quilt in any direction to create the stitching lines. A darning foot on a spring helps to accomplish this by giving some control of the layers, while allowing the sewer to create an infinite number of patterns to enhance the quilt surface. It takes practice to improve when using either method. I find free-motion to be more suited to my style of working. I can play all over the surface without having to lift and turn the quilt every few minutes. For me, turning the quilt around each time I change direction is not appealing; it is too much work.

Quilting is an exciting activity. I love watching the textures and patterns begin to form and bring the surface of my quilt to life. I hope you will also find the process as interesting as you gain proficiency at the same time!

Quilting is the act of sewing or tying together two or more layers of a quilt. Machine quilting is usually accomplished with an attachment called a walking foot or a darning foot. With a walking foot, most quilting motifs can be quilted by rotating or pivoting the quilt every time a direction change is needed. This method is well suited for long, straight, or gently curved lines. (For more information about darning feet, see page 23.)

Gallery

In 1988, I became a committed machine quilter. Working with beautiful shiny and variegated threads makes the time at my sewing machine more enjoyable. I particularly like to use threads that provide me with entertainment by changing color. The quilts in this gallery show a variety of techniques: patchwork, appliqué, free-motion embroidery, and beading; and all are machine quilted. (Illustrations of several machine-quilting motifs used on these quilts can be found in Quilting Motifs on pages 66–69.) In recent years I've reduced the amount of the embroidery on the quilts and increased the amount of a freestyle version of machine quilting that I call *dancing*.

WHISKERS, *Ann Fahl © 2006, 36½″ × 36″, wool batting*

WHISKERS

Oreo is looking right at the viewer with bright gold eyes. In this embroidered portrait I wanted to portray her whiskers as they glow when she sits in the sunshine. The hand-dyed green-to-turquoise background is quite plain, yet it provides a good contrast for the black and white. I chose a variegated green thread that blended both of the colors behind her head. It is always interesting to see how the different hues are highlighted as the thread crosses onto another background color. My choice for the quilting motif was a loop and leaf pattern for textural interest.

HAIRY HOMAGE

This quilt includes pieces leftover from previous cat quilts. Many are embroidered over a simple patchwork background. The large blue block includes the names of all my cats prior to Oreo. They all enriched my life by adding affection, humor, and cat hair. On this quilt are embroidered cats, computer-printed photos, and text. The heavy machine quilting was done with a playful feeling, using a variegated thread of red, yellow, blue, and green. Each segment of the quilt is quilted in a different way, to carry out the theme of scraps. I just quilted whatever I wanted to at the moment. It's fun to be spontaneous. In a way this could be called a quilting sampler.

HAIRY HOMAGE, *Ann Fahl © 2006, 35″ × 32½″, wool batting*

NOVEMBER GARDEN, *Ann Fahl © 2005, 50″ × 56″, wool batting*

NOVEMBER GARDEN

This quilt is a big change in color choice for me. Quiet, somber tones of gray and brown show off the silhouettes of the seed heads that remain in my garden in November. There is heavy machine embroidery using dark thread and metallics covering the leaves, stems, and seed heads. If you look closely there is a bubble or rock motif in the center of the larger seed pods. The quilting in the background is meant to give texture and a sense of air movement to the light gray, hand-painted fabric. The border of the pieced triangles is densely covered with branches of leaves and stippling, stitched in a solid, light gray thread. From a distance the viewer of this quilt sees the bold silhouettes of the plants. When stepping closer they can enjoy all the subtleties of all the quilting. I like giving my quilts interest at different levels. There is something for every viewer to enjoy.

WOW THAT'S ORANGE!

This quilt exudes light, warmth, and energy; my creative spirit is energized just by looking at it. The large, bright flowers and leaves are covered with free-motion embroidery. The flower centers were cut from a commercial print with lime green dots that make the quilt glow. The dots were outlined with quilting to make them stand out even more. The background of the quilt is full of surprises: there are quilted scallops around the flower centers, branches of leaves, and coneflowers blooming in the large empty spaces. The border quilting uses half of a flower shape that grows out of the fused double border. I echoed the shape over and over until the width of the border was full.

WOW THAT'S ORANGE! *Ann Fahl © 2006, 59½″ × 64″, wool batting*

ORANGE CONEFLOWERS, *Ann Fahl © 2006, 54˝ × 43½˝, wool batting*

ORANGE CONEFLOWERS

Here's more orange! These two oversized flowers were lifted from *Wow That's Orange!* The shadowed areas were embroidered onto the surface of the flowers with a variegated blue thread. The cones were created by layering yellow to lime green fabrics and accenting them with fused purple and red dots. Each flower is oversized, measuring about 36 inches across.

The quilting on the flowers creates small cell-like units on the petals because I needed something very simple to cover a huge area. In the bright blue background I used a variation of the seashell pattern that I opened up so it is just an echoed curved line that changes directions with a solid, bright blue thread. The single, large green leaf was detailed with a satin stitch. The quilting in each segment is filled with solid green thread stitched in undulating lines that create little veins on the surface.

A QUILTER'S MENAGERIE, *Ann Fahl © 2008, 61½˝ × 62½˝, wool batting*

A QUILTER'S MENAGERIE

This quilt is inspired by ancient Egyptian art, but it isn't as obvious. This is a fig tree, one of their many symbols of life and fertility, which has become my personal tree of life. In this composition you will find symbols and images that I have used in my quilting life: a swan, a heron, black-eyed Susans, coneflowers, a ginkgo leaf, my cat Oreo, water lilies, a dragonfly, and spirals. The little vine with white flowers that grows through the quilt is *Clematis paniculata,* which blooms every year on my deck.

My plan was for the machine quilting to continue the tree and leaf theme. So, in the body of the quilt I used a leaf and loop pattern to fill the spaces around the branches and embroidered leaves. I used many different solid and variegated green threads to enhance the richness of the hand-dyed background. Under the birds and flowers I quilted the circular rocks pattern to create a surface for them to rest on. The outer border has branches of leaves that cut diagonally across the edge, and you will see an occasional spiral that represents my spiral rose quilts of the 1990s. The remaining areas are filled with a twist-and-loop design.

ON THE NILE

Imagery from ancient Egypt has fascinated me for years. Egyptian images and wall paintings have reached out to me across the centuries, and I have interpreted them in fabric. This quilt is the most spiritual piece I've ever made. A pieced pyramid is in the background, with the Nile in the foreground. The stylized papyrus on the right (interpreted in pastel fabrics and gold thread) was inspired by an image on a gold box in the King Tut exhibit. The herons are fishing in the river, where many fish are swimming below. The backs of the birds are covered with variegated blue thread to imitate the feathers.

The quilting took an amazing amount of time. I thought it took a long time to piece the pyramid; it took much longer to quilt it. I created a jagged stitch to use on the sides of the pyramids. Using three different variegated brown threads, I spent days and hours filling the stone with my jagged stitch. The ridges in the sand were created by stitching repeated curved lines, using a solid rust-colored thread. Using a slightly darker color thread makes the area look richer, and it subtly enhances the stitching. If a lighter shade had been chosen, the quilting would not be as obvious.

I love quilting the scales on a fish. Before I quilt, they are just simple flat shapes fused onto the water. Using a strong turquoise thread for the clamshells and details of the faces and fins, they come to life when they are quilted. This is one of the little rewards that occur during the quilting process.

ON THE NILE, *Ann Fahl © 2007, 62½˝ × 45½˝, wool batting*

EGYPTIAN GARDEN I, *Ann Fahl © 2008, 65″ × 44½″, wool batting*

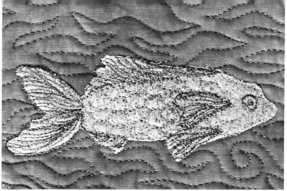

EGYPTIAN GARDEN I

Royal and wealthy Egyptians loved water gardens where they could sit, relax, and enjoy the cool water and lush green plants. My love of Winona Lake, Indiana, and my childhood summers there have always drawn me to water. I love the sound of the water and the wonderful cooling feeling that surrounds me when I jump in. This is why paintings of these ancient gardens really reach out to me.

Ponds were historically surrounded by date palms, doum palms, sycamore figs, kumquat trees, and pomegranate trees. The flowers here are poppies, cornflowers, lotus, papyrus, and mandrake fruit. Geese, ducks, and fish are swimming in the pond. The cartouche in the upper left corner includes my initials, AHF. The actual fragment that inspired this quilt is from the tomb of Nebamun, in the collection of the British Museum in London.

I enjoyed making all the detailed elements of this quilt, and I knew it would be fun to quilt. I outlined all the little details with monofilament first, then I danced with thread all over the surface of this quilt. The empty areas are full of all kinds of motifs that I have blended together. The fig and kumquat trees are filled with little leaves of variegated green. For the sky, I used turquoise variegated, purple variegated, or solid light turquoise thread, depending on the hue of the hand-dyed fabric; and I played, quilting however my heart desired. It is full of flowers, leaves, spirals, rocks, seashells, flames, wavy lines—you name it, it's in there. Likewise, the pond is full of texture, echoing, and clamshells. The fish in this pond were detailed in a pastel variegated thread and the fins with a blue variegated thread. Quilting was really enjoyable, very detailed, and took a long time for me to complete. It was worth every minute.

MESA VERDE: CLIFF PALACE, *Ann Fahl © 2008, 25½˝ × 24½˝, wool batting*

MESA VERDE: CLIFF PALACE

A trip to Mesa Verde National Park, with its wonderful bricks and ladders, inspired this quilt.

There is some embroidery on the ladders and vegetation on the right and lower edges to create detail. The bricks are quilted based on a rectangular shape—I went around the outside of each brick at least two times to give them a realistic, sculptured effect. I marked a small center area with pencil to get started, and the rest of the bricks were quilted freehand. To give the illusion of shading, I changed thread color, using the darkest for the brick outlines on the left and moving to the lightest beige on the right side.

I love this quilt and am very pleased with the final result, but the quilting wasn't as much fun as other quilts I've made. Nevertheless, I usually have an idea of how a piece should be quilted, and I always go with that feeling. I think I measure my success by the artful delivery of the appropriate style of quilting, not how much fun it was to complete. But as you've read, fun is important to me, too.

SUMMER SANCTUARY

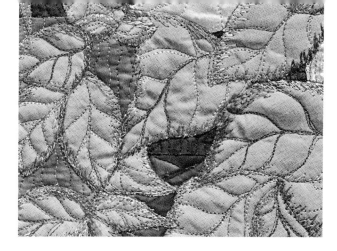

The summer depicted in this quilt was the year that the sixth *Harry Potter* book was published. The quilt shows my reading chair on the landing of our deck—the only shady spot. I took a photo of the setting on a steamy day in July, and that is how this quilt got its start.

The quilting is very heavy across the entire quilt—I danced all over the rich green background, adding as many leaves and loops as I could squeeze in. The quilting in the chair follows its contours and provides some shading. The wood grain on the floor of the deck was a long, stretched-out stipple using a neutral variegated thread. The actual quilting around the leaves and geraniums is just an outline with monofilament thread. On the outside edges I used the same branch of leaves and stipple that I used on the border of *November Garden* (page 10).

After the quilting was finished, I wasn't pleased with the quilt. The scene I had spent months on didn't have the same appeal as my original photo. After discussions with my critique group, I added Oreo for bold black-and-white contrast. I embroidered her on a separate piece of fabric, lightly appliquéd her on top of my finished quilt, and quilted around her with monofilament. She adds the punch that the quilt needed, and no doubt she will make it more difficult for me to read!

SUMMER SANCTUARY, *Ann Fahl © 2009, 48˝ × 52½˝, Tuscany wool batting*

TRILLIUM IN THE SUN

Trillium, with small white flowers, fill the woods in my yard. As they begin to fade, they turn a lovely soft pink. These trillium are extremely oversized to create strong visual impact. A real trillium is only 2–3 inches across, and these are 16–25 inches. I love the strong contrast of the orange pieced background, with shades from dark orange at the upper right to yellow in the lower left.

The quilting on the petals gives a cell-like effect much like that in *Orange Coneflowers* (page 12). There is dancing all over the orange: I quilted spirals, wavy lines, leaves, stars, and seashells using solid orange thread. On the huge leaves I needed something special to offset their dull green color, so I covered them with spirals and wavy lines. It is so exciting to try something bold, and have it be successful. The leaves are almost as exciting to me as the orange background.

TRILLIUM IN THE SUN, *Ann Fahl © 2008, 43˝ × 43˝, wool batting*

TEA PARTY

The subject of tea comes up in my quilts from time to time. I find it quite soothing to drink a hot cup of tea, especially when it's cold outside. I even pack a small teapot in my suitcase when I travel so I can feel some of the comforts of home and relax.

The figures on this quilt are fused in place and machine appliquéd. The quilting designs change with the area I am quilting. The teapot, doily, cups, and lemon are just lightly enhanced with lines that echo the shape. The quilting on the purple tabletop is covered with leaves growing on a fine stem using a luscious, variegated purple thread that helps to subtly enhance the quilting. Oreo is covered with little flowers with spiral centers in the white areas, and seashells in a dark variegated thread on the black areas. For the outside corners, I chose large leaves detailed with veins, surrounded with stippling in a blue variegated thread.

To be successful in blending many different quilting motifs to create the whole is one of my personal challenges. Here I used the very sizable leaves in the corners, a small stipple, medium-sized flowers and leaves, and echoed lines. By changing the scale, the quilting has more variety and is more interesting.

TEA PARTY, *Ann Fahl © 2006, 36˝ × 38˝, wool batting*

TRILLIUM IN TECHNICOLOR, *Ann Fahl © 2009, 43″ × 48½″, Tuscany wool batting*

TRILLIUM IN TECHNICOLOR

The five large trillium are appliquéd onto a pastel patchwork background. I love how the quilting appears on a softer background with its shadows and highlights, and the environment it provides for the wildflowers. The stems and leaves are made from a purple overdyed fabric that provides dramatic contrast to the soft background.

The background quilting is quite heavy, using a small trillium flower, spirals, and leaves. The quilting of seashells and curved lines on the leaves is done with a dark variegated thread that seems to sing on the surface. The quilting on the flowers is similar, using variegated threads that blend with the petal color. There is no fabric border, but the subtle quilting on the outside edge suggests one. The wavy vertical-line border pattern fills in the undulating spaces between the edge and the trillium pattern in the center.

PAINTED GARDEN, *Ann Fahl © 2008, 13½˝ × 13½˝, wool batting*

PAINTED GARDEN

For at least three years I saved this beautiful scrap of hand-painted cotton. It was waiting for a special subject. Before Christmas I decided that I'd embroider a spray of leaves over it, but instead of leaves, I placed my favorite coneflowers and black-eyed Susans on it. Because of the rich color of the background, I chose very rich but not quite realistic colors for the flowers and leaves.

In my usual fashion, I embroidered the flowers and leaves, and felt quite pleased with the way it looked. I thought about the quilting for quite awhile, waiting for the right idea, and after the holidays I spent parts of three days dancing all over the background. It was a lot of fun but required a lot of concentration on my part because the spaces were so tiny. Instead of using my usual heavy decorative thread in the top, I used a much finer 60-weight Bottom Line bobbin thread, changing colors to match the background. The quilting is similar to that on *Egyptian Garden I* (pages 16–17); it's just on a smaller scale.

TRIANGLES AND BEADS II

Planning the machine quilting was a daunting task, because there was so little space between the iridescent bugle beads that form the curved floral design that radiates out from the square center. I spent a lot of time doodling with paper and pencil. Finally, I felt confident enough to start quilting. I am pleased with the final result, and learned the importance of having a *plan* for the quilting. It can be changed as you go along, but it helps to get started. This quilt uses every motif included in this book, plus more. There are leaves, scallops, seashells, clamshells, wavy lines, and spirals, with a narrow border of parallel lines. I really like the way the bold central design is enhanced by the heavy quilting with the variegated thread that can be enjoyed when viewed close-up.

TRIANGLES AND BEADS II, *Ann Fahl © 2003, 67˝ × 67˝, cotton blend batting*

TOOLS

If you've been quilting for a while, you probably own most everything you need for machine quilting, or dancing with thread.

Sewing Machine

A sewing machine is your most important tool. The features I like best are—

- large throat or opening
- needle up/down
- knee lift
- easy way to lower feed dogs
- easy way to adjust tension
- top pressure adjustment
- stitch length and width controls

A complex machine with many computer menu levels is *not* helpful for free-motion work because it takes so long to make simple adjustments. Spend a lot of time test-sewing a machine before buying one. In particular, make sure the darning foot is to your liking.

There are so many machine options available to quilters. I like to sit down while I sew and manipulate the quilt with my hands, so a home sewing machine is my preference. A good alternative is a midarm sewing machine: It allows you to sit down while you sew, it has a large opening, it sews fast, it has needle up/down, and the size and speed make this type of machine perfect for really large quilts. However, it is limited to free-motion work with a straight stitch; there isn't a zigzag or decorative stitch option. So, in my mind, a midarm would be purchased *in addition to* your regular machine. Whatever you choose, make sure it fits your needs. Take the time to make a list of what you need. When you are ready to go to the dealer for a "test drive," bring along the materials you commonly use when you sew. This is the only way to know if the machine suits you.

Darning Foot

A darning foot is specifically designed for free-motion work. The design differs with each manufacturer. Usually the foot has a round or oval base and is mounted on a flexible or spring attachment that allows the foot to move up and down with the motion of the needle. Check your machine manual or ask your dealer which foot is suitable for your machine. If the standard darning foot for your brand isn't to your liking, ask about alternatives or try some of the generic feet on the market.

Test the darning foot. Can you easily see where you are going? You will need to quilt in seamlines and around embellishments and appliqués. The larger the foot, the more visibility you have. Some styles are open in the front. This increases visibility, but the open toe can get tangled in the edge of the quilt or in the batting. I find I need two feet: an open foot for general quilting and a closed style for quilting the border. If you are testing a new machine, test the darning feet too. This might change your mind about which machine to purchase. It is that important.

Some of my students ask about a stitch regulator for their machines. In my workshops, I prefer that they leave them at home. The idea is a good one, but in reality, they hold you back. With just a little practice, you have more freedom to sew, quilt, or embroider as you want without it. Secondly, they are expensive and for the most part unnecessary. Purchase a machine with a good darning foot; you will be happier and save money, too.

Darning feet

Straight-Stitch Throat Plate

Machines that sew zigzag and decorative stitches have a throat plate that accommodates the widest swing of the needle. For straight and free-motion stitching and quilting, you'll get a better quality stitch with a straight-stitch throat plate that has a small hole, just big enough for the needle. Check with a sewing store that carries your brand of machine to see if you can get one.

Sewing Machine Table

The sewing table should offer you a large flat surface. If the sewing machine can be built into the table or be level with the table surface, the job of quilting will go so much smoother for you. There are commercially made tables in all price ranges that are adaptable for all sizes of machines.

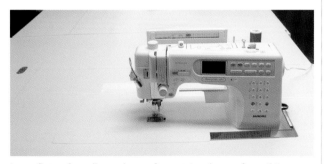

Large flat surface allows plenty of unrestricted space for quilting. *Photo by Ann Fahl*

Lighting for the Sewing Machine

As we age, we need more light to accomplish the same task than we did ten years ago. Some sewing machine models offer two or three light bulbs built into the machine to help us see where we are stitching. I always need more. I've used desk lamps and clamp-on types to try to better illuminate the needle area.

The Bendable Bright Light (see Resources, page 95) is very liberating. It is so tiny that you hardly know it's there. It doesn't block machine controls and allows you to sew with great visibility. Use whatever combination of lighting that you have available to flood the needle area with light.

Tiny lamp aims light just where you need it. *Photo by Ann Fahl*

Iron or Steamer

For a successful, professional appearance you can be proud of, it is important to steam the project at various stages of construction. An iron must have a steam feature with a powerful burst. This is very helpful in blocking your quilts (pages 40–44). I like a lot of steam when I piece, appliqué, and embroider.

A steamer is also a great tool. Most have a large water tank that can provide an almost endless supply of steam for large projects. The steamer itself can sit in the middle of the quilt, and the ironlike steam head will gently shoot a lot of steam into the quilt.

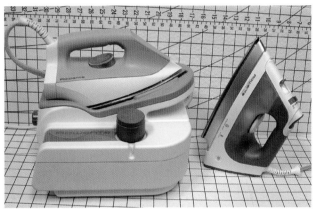

Good steam iron is essential for successful quilting; steamer helps during blocking process. Dressmaker's cutting board has a grid for squaring up when blocking. *Photo by Ann Fahl*

Dressmaker's Cutting Board

A dressmaker's cutting board is a folded cardboard surface that opens to 40 inches by 60 inches. A grid is printed on one side, which is used to press or steam projects to make sure they are square. Detailed use of this board is explained on pages 41–44.

Digital Camera and Printer

A digital camera and printer can be very helpful. You can photograph your quilt top and print it to help decide what quilting motifs to use. More details can be found on page 37.

Personal Notebook of Quilting Designs

This notebook cannot be purchased in any store—you must collect all the information yourself. It can be a file folder or a big three-ring binder that holds all your notes, sketches, and ideas for quilting. Why do this? Sometimes I have a new quilt top and the time to work on it, but no ideas on how to quilt it. By referring to my notebook, I just have to flip through the pages to find one. As I'm sewing, I keep my notebook open to the pages that are most appropriate.

My notebook began as a collection of loose pages of book covers, napkins, and tea bag wrappers, which I still have! Eventually the collection graduated to a pocket folder. Now I've gone really professional: I use a three-ring binder with page protectors. This allows me to save the original idea or sketch and notes by slipping it right in the clear protector. It's really easy to flip through my increasingly large collection of pages to find just the right thing for my next quilt.

Where do you get pages and ideas for your personal quilting notebook? There are many books on the market and in the library that contain continuous line or machine-quilting designs. Sketch the ones you like. Keep photos of quilts that have interesting ideas. Save advertisements and pages from magazines that contain patterns. Some websites have free pattern downloads. When you go to a quilt show, keep a small notebook or pad of paper handy so that you can sketch a pattern that appeals to you.

You don't have many sketches or ideas? Look through old magazines, and tear out the pages and photos that you like. Ideas can be found by looking at artwork in museums or even in your favorite fast-food restaurant.

I asked all the members of my quilting group to bring two quilting ideas to the following month's meeting. I assembled them all into a little booklet and gave everyone a copy. So, go out and collect ideas—you can never have too many pages in your book.

Have you started your notebook yet? What are you waiting for? If your ideas are all collected into one place, all you have to do is flip through the pages to find the right one. This collection doesn't have to be fancy; it just needs to be accessible. It will become your most important reference.

Here is a page from my notebook. I've included an envelope back with variations of spirals and small sketches of other interesting fill stitches.

SUPPLIES

An understanding of some smaller items will help the job of machine quilting go more smoothly.

Quilter's Gloves

Quilter's gloves make the job of quilting much easier on your hands. I was surprised how much more control they give than just bare hands. There are several types of gloves on the market—wear whatever type you prefer. Usually I wear a glove on each hand, but if the task requires changing thread colors often, I will wear a glove on my left hand, and change the thread with my bare right hand. The more you quilt, the more you can streamline and simplify your quilting process. Gloves really make a difference.

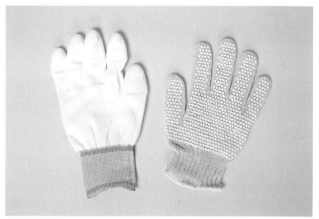

Wearing gloves makes quilting easier on hands.

SewSlip

This is a heavy vinyl sheet that covers the bed of the sewing machine and a little bit beyond. SewSlip provides a slick, smooth surface that does two things: First, it allows the sewer to move the quilted project with ease; and second, it smoothes out the levels of the machine, throat plate, table insert, and table, so that nothing can catch on the different levels. This product seems really simple, but it makes the job of free-motion go smoothly.

The SewSlip sheet is made of very clingy or electrostatic material designed so that it will not move or shift under the quilt. There is no need to tape it into position. To clean it, just rinse it under running water.

SewSlip makes free-motion quilting easier.

Small Scissors

Small scissors for snipping are essential for keeping the project free of thread. Even if there is a built-in thread cutter on your machine, the scissors will do a better job of keeping the back "string free." My favorite type has curved blades.

Safely clip threads using small scissors with curved blades.

Sewing Machine Needles

Needles create every stitch! We overlook the importance of machine needles because they are so small. For quilting with decorative threads, *topstitch* needles work better than all the other needles on the market. They have the largest eye and a channel machined into the shaft of the needle that protects the thread while the stitches are being made. These needles will put an end to shredding thread. For help in selecting the proper thread and needle sizes, see the chart on page 30.

I have found a way to simplify and reduce the number and types of needles I keep on hand. Keep these general guidelines in mind:

- Universal needles are good for piecing and general construction.
- Topstitch needles are essential for embroidery and quilting with all decorative thread.

Keep both types of needles nearby. For piecing I use 75/11 universals, and for embroidery and quilting I use 80/12–100/16 topstitch needles. As a reminder of what needle is in the machine, keep the needle case near the machine.

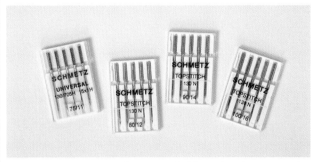

Two types of machine needles are needed for quiltmaking: topstitch and universal.

Marking Pencils

A lead pencil will help keep you on track by marking special features of your desired quilting designs. I use either a regular number 2 HB pencil for light-colored fabrics or a white or silver pencil for darks.

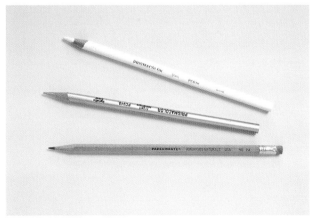

Mark quilt top with pencil.

Decorative Thread *and* Bobbins

THREAD

The thread used for quilting can make the surface of the project more interesting. Decorative thread is my favorite choice. Decorative thread is a little heavier than regular sewing thread, and I prefer one that is really shiny. Over the years, I have collected as many colors and varieties as possible. Because most of the fabrics I use have a flat finish, shiny threads show up beautifully and enhance the quilting designs.

As I teach threadwork around the country, I find a slight resistance to quilting threads other than cotton! There are so many beautiful types of thread on the market, why do some quilters resist using them? Watch dancers performing on the stage. They wear clothes with rhinestones and sequins to enhance their performance. Would the performance have the same look if the dancers wore denim? Why use cotton thread when rayon and polyester have such a beautiful glow? Highlight your work—make it shine! Make the quilting reflect your effort!

Darker stitching on left is cotton thread; rayon thread is on right side. Look closely; each stitch of rayon has reflective shine.

Decorative Thread

Decorative thread is different from standard cotton and polyester sewing threads. It is meant to be beautiful, colorful, and ornamental. These threads give a subtle glow to the stitching, which contrasts with the matte finish of quilt cotton.

Use regular-weight cotton, polyester, or polyester blend thread for piecing and hand appliqué. Decorative threads are more delicate than utility sewing threads. Don't use them for piecing or mending, because they are not strong enough for stitching seams. When

Decorative threads

storing thread, keep the two types in two separate containers.

I think of decorative threads in terms of two categories: solid color or variegated. Solid color thread is consistently the same hue throughout the entire spool. Variegated thread comes in two types:

- Single-color variegated thread is one hue with different variations, such as light to dark blue, or a combination of blues with the same theme, such as cornflower blue, turquoise, marine blue, and navy.

- Multicolor variegated thread includes several hues from the color wheel. One of my favorites flows in a rotation of red, purple, blue, green, yellow, and orange. This type comes in a large array of color choices.

Most thread manufacturers make variegated threads. The length of the color differs with the manufacturer—some change color every inch, others change about every 20 inches. Neither is better than the other. I use both types. The color is the most important factor in my decision making.

Why choose variegated? Because it offers more surface interest than a solid color thread. I personally find the process of quilting to be more interesting if the thread changes color.

If there are huge empty areas that need to be quilted, a multicolor variegated thread may be just what you need. If the quilting space is quite small, a single color variegated or a solid color might be a better choice.

Variegated thread adds interest to quilt surface.

Metallic Thread

Metallic thread is a way to add some sparkle to your work. Sometimes quilting with metallic thread will go smoothly, and other times it can be very challenging. Metallics are more delicate than other decorative threads. This thread comes in two types:

- Twisted metallics have several plies that are twisted together like most traditional threads.

- Flat metallics are the most reflective and the most challenging to sew with. Be careful when using a hot iron near them; some of them might melt. Avoid piercing lines of flat metallic stitching with a machine needle, because this will cause the stitches to break.

Metallic thread

Tips for Quilting *with* Metallic Threads

- Stitch more slowly.

- Use a 90/14 topstitch needle or larger.

- Loosen the upper tension (page 31).

- Flat-wound metallics should sit on an upright pin. Cross-wound spools should sit sideways or feed off a thread stand.

- Use a smooth thread in the bobbin, such as The Bottom Line (page 32).

- Flat metallic thread should be the very last thread used in the quilting process.

- Try using a liquid silicone product to keep stitches from skipping. Sewers Aid (by Collins; see Resources, page 95) is one brand that is effective. Check with the sewing machine manufacturer regarding its use.

Choosing the Right Thread

When I decide on a thread, not only does it have to be shiny, but it has to be the appropriate color. Unwind about 36 inches of the thread, and let it puddle on the fabric or quilt. Do you like it? If not, then select another thread, and do the same thing. If you still aren't sure, then sew with each possible thread on a small sample of the same fabric. Place your sample on the quilt. Is it the right one? If not, try another until you have found the right one.

Auditioning thread

Take Time to Find *the Right* Quilting Thread

Taking the time to stitch a small sample using your thread choice may seem time-consuming, but it is worth the time if you are unsure. I've learned that ten minutes of quilting can take hours to remove, so make sure you make the correct choice the first time. Ask me how I know.

Thread Sizing and Needle Selection

Understanding the sizing system will help you choose the appropriate needle for your quilting. Everyone has experienced thread shredding or breaking at the eye of the needle. This is a very frustrating experience for the beginner. There is a simple solution: You must use a needle that is appropriate for the thread. If the thread in the machine is heavy, it will break if the eye of the needle is too small. If the thread is fine and you have a large needle, you will be punching unnecessarily large holes with every stitch. The chart below will help you choose the correct needle size.

THE THREAD AND NEEDLE CONNECTION

Thread size	Ann's weight designation	Decorative thread type	Needle type and suggested size*
20-weight	Very heavy	Metallic, metallic blends, polyester	Topstitch 100/16
30-weight	Heavy	Polyester, rayon, metallic	Topstitch 100/16
35-weight	Medium	Twisted or tweed rayon	Topstitch 90/14
40-weight	Medium	Most rayon, polyester, metallic	Topstitch 80/12, 90/14
50-weight	Fine	Cotton, polyester	Universal 75/11
60-weight	Very fine	Cotton, polyester	Universal 70/10, 75/11
Monofilament	Extra-fine	Nylon, polyester	Universal 75/11 or smaller

Always test stitch the thread with the smallest possible needle size. If shredding occurs, move to the next larger size needle.

Simplify Your Needle Choice

One of the most common problems is that quilters use the wrong size or type of needle. To simplify your selection, I only keep two types of machine needles on hand.

UNIVERSAL NEEDLES have a small eye and are great for piecing, clothing construction, and general sewing.

TOPSTITCH NEEDLES have a much larger eye and a channel above the eye—delicate threads can be protected while the needle goes up and down through all the layers—so they are the perfect choice for stitching with decorative threads.

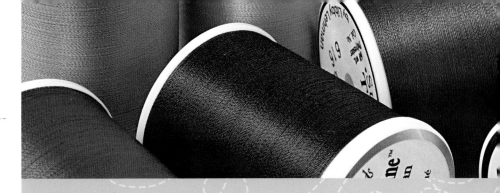

Adjusting the Top Tension

After the machine has been threaded, test the stitches first on a small batting sandwich. Is the stitch balanced on both sides? Each stitch should be rounded to be perfect. If not, the first thing to do is to rethread both the top and the bobbin, making sure the presser foot is in the *up* position.

What Adjustments Need to Be Made?

- If small loops are showing on the back side—tighten the top tension.

- If small loops are showing on the top—loosen the top tension.

- If the thread seems to be tight or pulling on the top—loosen top tension, make sure the machine is threaded properly, or move the quilt more slowly while stitching faster.

- If the stitches on the back are poorly formed and bobbin thread appears to be very tight—tighten top tension slightly, or move the quilt more slowly while stitching faster. It's also possible that the bobbin tension may be too tight or not feeding properly (page 32).

Ann's Top Ten Thread Tips

When experiencing problems with thread or quilting stitches, try these tips.

1. Make sure the presser foot is *up* when threading the machine.

2. Completely remove the top thread and the bobbin, and rethread the machine. Decorative threads are slippery and can slip out of the tension disks or plates.

3. Experiment with the tension settings. With decorative thread, loosening is necessary. Lower the tension setting by one number, test, and continue lowering the tension by one number until the shredding or breaking stops.

4. Try a new needle. Do you need a larger size, or is the needle damaged? Change it every 6–8 hours of sewing.

5. Change the position of the spool or cone of thread. If the spool is parallel wound, it should sit on a vertical pin, and the thread should reel off from the side. If it is cross-wound (you will see a pattern of X's), it should be placed either on a thread stand or on a horizontal pin, and the thread should reel off from the top.

Parallel and cross-wound thread

6. Use a thread stand or thread net to keep thread from twisting, puddling, or knotting.

7. Always test the machine stitch on a scrap of fabric after you've changed the needle, bobbin, or thread.

8. If bobbin thread is making loops on top, tighten the tension of the bobbin. Check your machine manual for instructions.

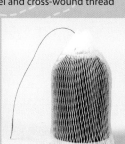

Thread net prevents thread from twisting and knotting.

Thread stand allows thread to feed evenly.

9. When all else fails, turn off the machine, wait ten seconds so it can reset itself. Then power up the machine again.

10. Take a break.

Volumes can be written about thread. For more detailed information, please refer to my book *Coloring with Thread* (C&T Publishing).

BOBBINS

Bobbins control half of every stitch the machine makes. Pay more attention to how the stitches appear on the back of your quilt. For quilting, I use two types of thread in my bobbin: monofilament and Bobbinfil.

Monofilament Thread

Monofilament is an extra-fine thread made of nylon or polyester. Today, it is a soft flexible thread that can hardly be seen when used in the bobbin for quilting. I have used this successfully for years. It is available in clear for light colors and smoke for medium to dark fabrics. Every quilter needs a spool of both colors.

Monofilament is available in clear and smoke.

Bobbinfil Thread

Bobbinfil thread was created to be a smooth, fine thread. Because it is so fine, more of it will fit in the bobbin than regular-weight sewing thread. As you quilt you'll find that it makes life easier, because the bobbin doesn't have to be changed as often.

The Bottom Line brand from Superior Threads (see Resources, page 95) is a fine, smooth polyester thread that is 60-weight. It comes in a large selection of colors and is wonderful in the bobbin for machine quilting and embroidery. It is a more stable thread than the monofilament, because it doesn't stretch. It leaves very little lint in the bobbin case too. Since I started using it, I've found how versatile it is. It can be used in the top of the machine for quilting, and it can be used for hand appliqué and hemming.

Bobbin thread is extremely fine and comes in many colors to match or blend with decorative thread.

Why Use Bobbin Thread?

Bobbin thread makes it possible to get many more yards of thread in the bobbin. If you use regular-weight thread, it seems that the bobbin empties often and you have to put in another. Using bobbin thread is a time-saver and is less conspicuous on the quilt back.

Adjusting the Bobbin Tension

Bobbin threads are not only fine but also quite smooth and slippery. Usually it is necessary to make some adjustments because they have a tendency to pull quickly out of the bobbin, causing loops to show on the top of your work.

If you own a Bernina machine, this can be remedied by putting the thread through the hole in the arm that extends out of the bobbin case. Some Bernina machines have the option of using a gold bobbin case. Instead of an arm, there is a little clip or spring that the thread can be slipped under. Janome now offers a free-motion quilting foot and bobbin holder set that has the bobbin tension set for free-motion work.

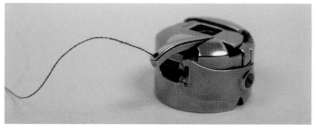

Bernina bobbin case

The rest of us need to adjust the little screw on the side of the bobbin case. This is something that your home economics teacher told you never to do. But we are quilters and can safely do this. Check your machine manual to locate the tiny screw that regulates the tension. Place a tiny dot with a permanent marker where the slot on the head of the screw is pointed. With a small screwdriver, turn *right* to tighten or *left* to loosen the bobbin tension. When you are finished sewing, you can turn the bobbin screw back to its original setting where you made the mark.

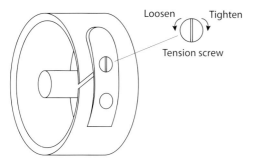

Bobbin case

Here is another way to check the bobbin tension. There should be some resistance when the bobbin thread is pulled through the case. If it comes out freely, tighten it until you feel some resistance.

If you feel some resistance when pulling thread, tension is correct.

If your machine has a drop-in bobbin, there is a way to change the bobbin tension. Check your machine manual first. Remove the throat plate and lift out the bobbin case, adjust the screw, and reposition it in the machine. This is fairly simple. When you are finished, remember to return the bobbin case tension to its original factory setting.

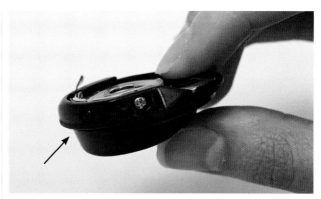

Adjustment screw on Janome drop-in bobbin case

Keep an *Extra* Bobbin Case on Hand

Because both monofilament and The Bottom Line are very fine threads, the bobbin tension may need to be adjusted. I suggest that you consider purchasing an *extra bobbin case* so that you can have one case set at factory settings and the other case set for finer bobbin thread.

Winding Bobbin Thread on the Bobbin

Some machine users will experience problems winding this fine thread on the bobbin. It will wrap itself under the bobbin while winding, or loops and other problems will arise. This is easily remedied by simply pinching the thread lightly between your thumb and forefinger before it winds on the bobbin, guiding slightly as the bobbin fills up. This puts extra tension on the thread so it will wind smoothly.

Because bobbin thread is so fine, it may need your attention while winding.

Batting *and* Backing

CHOOSING THE RIGHT BATTING

Although we don't spend much time looking at or thinking about batting, it is an important part of a quilt. It provides the dimension, loft or "puff," that makes the surface of the quilt come alive. In a bed quilt, it provides the warmth.

There are so many types of batting on the market that a thorough discussion could fill a book. Batting can be purchased in pure white, natural, and black. The fibers commonly found in batting are cotton, wool, polyester, bamboo, and silk.

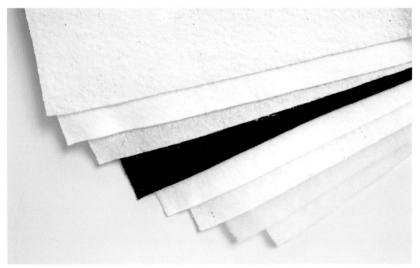

Batting

Take the time to make samples of your quilting using different types of batting. This will help you decide which type will give you the look, feel, and drape that you desire.

Ask your quilting friends to give you a sample of the battings they like best, and make samples that are 12- to 24-inch squares.

I tested six types of batting, making a 6-inch square of the same cotton fabric as the quilt top and backing. I quilted a similar pattern on each sample. What I found was that a larger sample is really needed to show the differences between the batting fibers!

This chart includes my own findings and opinions. I did not test every batting available, so it doesn't represent everything on the market today. My statements are generally true. If you make a few samples of batting as suggested, you will be able to make an informed decision about which batting to use.

For my art quilts I prefer the loft that wool batting provides because my quilts are heavy with thread work. The Tuscany Wool batting provides the highest quality and most consistent loft of any on the market.

When you complete a quilt, remember to list the type of batting used on the label stitched to the back. Also list it in your journal or inventory because you will never remember a year from now what you put inside. This is important information that will be needed when it's time to clean the quilt.

Small quilted samples of different battings

ANN'S BATTING CHOICES FOR MACHINE QUILTING

Batting type	Thickness of batting	Ann's "puff quotient"	Manufacturer recommended quilting interval	Bearding*	Washability and shrinkage**	Available in dark color	Additional info
Fleece—polyester batting; densely packed fiber	Thin	Low	6"–10"	Minimal	Machine wash; no shrinkage	No	Good choice for heavily used and washed quilts; low loft appropriate for placemats and table runners
Polyester	Thin, medium, or high	Medium to high	2"–8"	Minimal to moderate	Machine wash; no shrinkage	No	Gives soft, puffy appearance; bearding can be undesirable; high lofts difficult to manipulate through opening in sewing machine
100% Cotton	Thin	Low	2"	Minimal	Washable; check manufacturer's instructions for care; 3–5% shrinkage	No	Handle carefully, especially when removing from package; soft hand; lightweight; antique look when finished quilt is washed
Cotton blend	Thin to medium	Low	2"–4"	None to minimal	Washable; some shrinkage	Yes	Good choice for machine quilting due to lower loft; easier to manipulate through sewing machine
Wool	Medium	High	4"	None to minimal	Check manufacturer's instructions for washing; no shrinkage	Yes	Lightweight with high resiliency; makes quilting pattern highly visible
Silk blend	Thin	Medium	4"	None to minimal	Hand wash; air dry; 5% shrinkage	No	Highest cost
Bamboo	Thin	Low	8"	None to minimal	Machine wash; 2–3% shrinkage	No	Environmentally green product; naturally anti-bacterial; very soft hand to finished quilt

*Batting fibers migrate through quilt top, creating a hairy appearance.
**Always follow manufacturer's suggestion.

Batting Challenges

If you choose a batting with high loft, or your quilt is not properly basted, you may experience some quilt top movement. As you sew, you will find bubbles of extra quilt top developing that need to be pushed out to the edges. Always quilt from the center out, as evenly as you can. If you find yourself sewing in the opposite direction, you may develop puckers or little pleats. This can be controlled by pressing down with both hands and lightly pulling your hands apart as you quilt (page 45).

Shifting quilt top creates little bubbles of excess quilt top.
Photo by Ann Fahl

Solving the Creased Batting Problem

The biggest problem with batting is that it is heavily creased when removed from the package. There are several ways to solve this.

- Take it out of the package, and unroll it at least one day before basting.

- If appropriate to the fiber content, lightly mist the crushed batting with water, and tumble in the dryer at an appropriate setting or let it air dry.

- Purchase batting by the yard at your favorite retailer.

- Use premium battings for higher quality.

CHOOSING THE RIGHT QUILT BACKING

There are two things to consider when choosing the right fabric for the back of your quilt: color and thread count. I prefer a fabric whose color blends with the design on the quilt top. If the fabric is printed or has a mottled look, it will help camouflage minor stitching problems.

Over the years I've learned that there are some fabrics that are not appropriate for use on the back.

- Fabrics with a really high thread count make it difficult to sew through and cause your thread to shred. How can you tell if the thread count is too high? Try pulling a thread or two off the cut edge of the yardage. If it pulls off easily, it is okay to use. If it is really difficult to pull a thread across the width, leave it on the shelf.

- Some surface treatments may shred your thread as you quilt. Avoid fabrics with paint on them—white-on-cream prints and gold or other metallic paint will make your job more difficult. Fabric with a high-gloss finish such as chintz is difficult to work with. These are best left for other projects.

Choosing *and* Marking Quilting Designs

HOW TO CHOOSE A QUILTING MOTIF OR DESIGN

When I talk about quilting designs, motifs, and patterns, I am referring to the decorative stitching used to sew all the layers together.

Make a Sample

How would you like to quilt the open areas of your quilt? This is where your quilting design notebook (page 25) comes in handy. Flip through your collection of sketches and ideas, and pick out several you'd like to try. I would suggest that you make a small quilt sandwich with two pieces of your quilt fabric on either side of a piece of batting, and try out the quilting motifs that you think you'd like to use. A practice piece the size of a placemat (18″ × 12″) is large enough to give you plenty of practice. If you like the motif you've chosen, go ahead and use it to fill the background of your quilt.

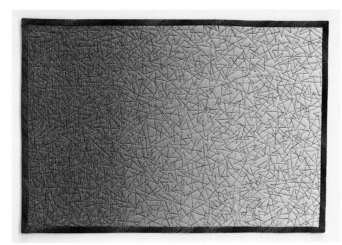

Make placemat-size practice pieces.

Take a Picture

If a quilt is complicated, large, or very special, I take a digital picture of it and print two to six copies of it in color on 8½-by-11-inch paper. Using a marker or ballpoint pen, I draw or doodle on the photos until I come up with a plan that I'm happy with. Since I've been a doodler my entire life, this works well for me.

Take the pages to your favorite coffee shop or a quiet place, other than your sewing area, and doodle away. You will be surprised what you can dream up when you leave your sewing area. When you've filled up your quilt pictures with marker, you will know when you've found the right idea or combination of ideas. It will have a good feel to it.

Preliminary sketches

Other Ideas

If you are still unsure, show your ideas to a quilting friend, and perhaps the two of you can come up with a plan. Take it one step at a time. Decide what you will do in the interior of the quilt, and then quilt it. When this is done, then you can consider what to do on the border. I find that as I stitch on a quilt, ideas begin to flow through my mind that help me decide on a pattern for the outside edge.

You might consider using a product called Quilter's Vinyl (see Resources, page 95), which is a heavy, clear product. Lay it over your photograph, and draw using washable markers or grease pencils that wipe off. Use whatever method works for you to find the right combination of quilting motifs for your project.

Just Start Quilting!

If you still are unsure of what to do, put the quilt top away. The right idea may come to you later. But if you've been waiting for the idea for a long time, it is time to stop delaying—just start. Ideas will come to mind if you begin stabilizing the quilt. Start with your favorite simple motif, and let the rest evolve as you work. No quilt top ever got finished while folded up in the closet!

HOW TO MARK A QUILT TOP

I do very little marking on my quilt top. There are a few exceptions. Usually I practice a motif or pattern on a sample and then begin quilting the same design on my quilt when I feel I'm ready. On some occasions I want a certain line, angle, or shape in a specific area of the quilt. With a marking pencil I lightly mark the area or place for that special design. Other times I will use a series of straight pins to mark an area for my stitching, blue painter's tape, or narrow ¼-inch quilter's tape. Whatever method you prefer is fine.

As you concentrate on filling in each area with a pattern, it's easy to forget the big picture. It can be helpful to mark guidelines to follow when a special effect is planned. So mark when needed; otherwise, just quilt as desired.

In *Wow That's Orange!* (page 11), I quilted large coneflowers into the large open areas above the garden. I marked the outline of the flower with just a light pencil line, and filled in more details as I stitched.

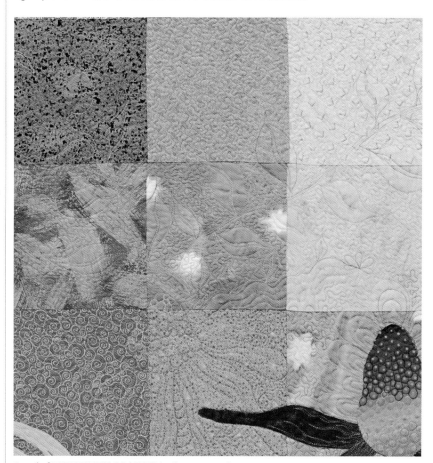

Detail of **WOW THAT'S ORANGE!** *(quilt on page 11)*

In *August Garden,* I wanted to put some featherlike vines growing in and around the flowers. Here I used a white pencil on the red background and drew long wavy lines that became the base for the feathers. Actually it is just seashells on both sides of a curvy line.

AUGUST GARDEN, *Ann Fahl © 2003, 49˝ × 49˝. Photo by Sharon Risedorph*

Quilted featherlike vines in *August Garden. Photo by Sharon Risedorph*

MARKING THE BORDERS

My advice for the border is the same as for the body of the quilt. Mark as little as possible, but when you have something special in mind, use pencil. On more than one occasion, I've made a small plastic or cardboard template to mark a special outline. It is easier to space evenly around the outside edge this way. If you'd like to use a special shell shape or repeat a shape from the inner portion of the quilt, do so, but do take care to space the motif evenly or in a way that balances the outside edges. Then dance in the remaining space with your favorite patterns.

Another note about borders: I completely fill the center portion of the quilt before I mark the border. As I quilt the inside, sometimes I get an interesting idea for the border. So after the inside is finished, I mark the outside edges. It is possible to mark everything first before basting. But by the time you get to the border, the markings will have almost disappeared. So mark as the spirit moves you.

Paper pattern was used to mark positions of spirals on *A Quilter's Menagerie* (quilt on page 13).

Preparation *for* Quilting

CLEANING UP THE QUILT TOP

Before you go any further in the quilting process, take an hour or two to clean up the back of your quilt top. It is hard to make yourself do this, because you are anxious to get on to the basting and quilting. Seam allowances need to be trimmed where a darker fabric extends beyond a lighter seam, creating a shadow. Trim any loose threads. If you used stabilizer, remove as much of it as possible. Carefully check both the front and the back of the project. Lay it over the batting or white paper—this will show you where there may be shadowing of seams or anything else that needs to be addressed. You won't be sorry you spent the time. These little problems can't be fixed once the quilt has been basted or quilted.

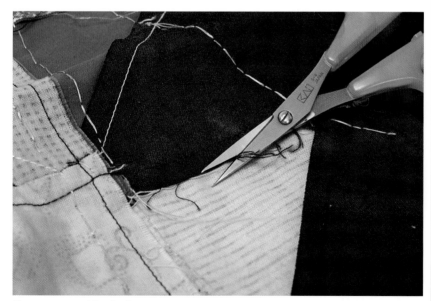

Clean up wrong side of quilt top.

BLOCKING

Before you can begin quilting, you need to block and baste the completed quilt top. Think of this process as being as important as preparing a room to be painted. Before you paint the room, you need to scrub stains and marks on the wall, fill nail holes, cover the furniture and floor, and put painter's tape on the trim. All this takes longer than painting the entire room. But the paint job will look much more professional if you've prepared everything first!

The idea is the same as making sure your quilt top is properly prepared to be quilted. I've found that my method of basting and blocking is the major reason my quilts hang so well on the wall and at quilt exhibits. Try blocking; I think you will agree.

In order for you to make a quilt that lies flat and square, you need to start with a top that is flat and square.

Blocking Supplies

To block a finished quilt top in preparation for quilting, you will need:

- dressmaker's cutting board
- straight pins
- curved safety pins
- tape measure about 8′ long
- good steam iron

The goal is to make sure the quilt top is square or has 90° corners. The grid on the dressmaker's cutting board is important for this.

What happens if the quilt is bigger than the cutting board? Actually I have six of them in my studio. I can fit two on my cutting table, butt them together, smooth out the fabric, and pin it in place. There is no need to use tape on the boards. If the quilt is really big, push as many boards together as needed. I use the floor of my living room for large quilts—I push the furniture back, put on clean socks, and walk on and around the quilt as I pin it on the boards.

To block quilts, use cutting board with grid, pins, tape measure, and steam iron. *Photo by Ann Fahl*

Pin the Top into Position

Line up the bottom edge of the quilt with the bottom line in the grid. Use straight pins to pin the edge of the block or quilt onto the grid every 3″–4″, or as needed. Next, pin the right edge. Pull and smooth the left side into position and pin. The top edge is the most difficult to get into line. Pull, and smooth into place as best you can and pin as often as needed.

Pin quilt top to grid. *Photo by Ann Fahl*

Insert pins with tips aimed toward center of quilt and heads angled away from center. *Photo by Ann Fahl*

Steam the Top

Set the iron for high steam. Steam the quilt while it is pinned in place. Let the iron hover above the surface. Let it dry completely. If there is still some distortion on the edges, steam and smooth the problem area with your hand and re-pin. Steam again. Do not trim any edges.

Hover with steam iron. *Photo by Ann Fahl*

Let It Dry

When the top feels dry to the touch, take out the pins, and remove the top from the dressmaker's cutting board.

Blocking is the best way to make a top absolutely square. The rigid, printed grid is a big help in lining up the edges while the steam relaxes the fibers into shape.

Now the top is ready to be basted.

A Quilt Can Be *Blocked* at Every Stage

- As patchwork blocks are completed
- Before a border is sewn around the center
- After the border is applied
- After embroidery or appliqué
- After machine quilting
- After packing and shipping—if a quilt is heavily creased during shipping, lay it out (without pinning edges), and steam heavily.

BASTING

Now that you've blocked and steamed the quilt top, you know it is square. It is time to baste all the layers together. The backing should be pieced, pressed, and checked to see that it is several inches larger (in both directions) than the quilt top.

Pin the Quilt Backing onto the Cutting Board

Pin the quilt backing, right side down, to the dressmaker's cutting board the same way you did with the top (page 41). The pins should be placed into the edge of the fabric and the cardboard, so the points of the pins are aimed toward the quilt center. It is important that the fabric be tight enough that there are no wrinkles.

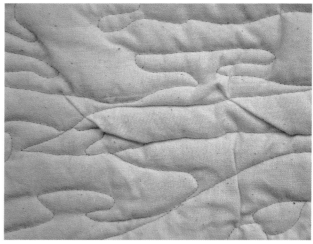

Pin quilt back so it is taut, eliminating tucks and pleats such as this on wrong side. *Photo by Ann Fahl*

Layer the Batting

Next, place the batting on top of the pinned backing. With scissors, trim the batting so it doesn't extend beyond the backing. Before proceeding to the next step, make sure the batting lies flat, without heavy creases, bumps, or bubbles. Smooth out the batting on top of the pinned backing, and mist it with a water bottle. Use a steam iron or steamer and hover above the batting so that the steam permeates the thickness. The batting will relax and dry. Also refer to Batting Challenges on page 36.

Pin the Top into Position

Carefully place the blocked quilt top on top of all the batting. Because the lines on the cardboard grid can't be seen, place the end of a tape measure on an edge of the cardboard, and pin it in place. Pull the measuring tape across to the other side of the board, and use this as a straight edge for pinning the quilt top in position.

The tape measure should be about 1″ inside the edge of the quilt top. As before, begin pinning on the bottom edge, and pin every 3″ or so, making sure the top is taut. Move the tape measure to the right side, and use it to align and pin the right edge. Do the same with the left side. Last, place the rule on the top edge, and pin the quilt top so it is straight.

Place tape measure 1″ inside edge of quilt top. *Photo by Ann Fahl*

I like to lightly steam all three layers a little, again letting the iron hover just above the surface. Steaming makes the layers cling together.

Baste with Safety Pins

Use rust-free safety pins (I like the big curved ones best), and pin the layers together while the outside edges are securely pinned into the cutting board. Start in the center of the quilt, and pin the layers together every 3″–6″. Try to insert the safety pins into seamlines or on the outside edges of appliqués so the holes are less likely to show when removed.

On the outside edges of the quilt, pin every 3″–4″.

Put safety pins through all three layers. *Photo by Ann Fahl*

What has been accomplished? All the layers have been aligned and pinned together so they will hold the 90° corners or square shape. This is *very important* to preserve the integrity of fabric, grain, and shape of the finished quilt.

Remove the straight pins from the outside edges of the layered and basted quilt. Now, quilt as desired. Don't you just love it when the instructions say that? For me, quilting is the most interesting part of the process—it creates dimension, highlights, shadows, and surface texture. It deserves as much thought and planning as the quilt top itself.

Blocking and basting isn't fun, but it is *worth the effort!* Turn on your favorite music to help speed you along. Have your favorite beverage at hand, and maybe invite a friend to help you make this task more enjoyable!

For *Easier* Basting

Curved 1½-inch safety pins make the job of pin-basting easier on your hands.

BLOCKING THE FINISHED QUILT

Blocking the finished quilt is much the same process as discussed earlier (page 40–42). When all the layers are machine quilted, the quilt has been twisted, turned, stitched, and filled with quilting. In the process, you have distorted the quilt—*don't worry*. If you basted the layers together and steamed it, it will return to its square or rectangular shape again. The following is how it's done.

Pin the Edges

Pull out the dressmaker's cutting board and tape measure again. First, pin the bottom edge of the quilt with pins, using the measuring tape as a guide.

Next, hook the tape measure on the right edge, and smooth and pin the quilt into position. Do the same with the left side. The top or the last side is the most difficult; push, pull, or smooth the fabric, and pin.

Pin quilt for blocking. *Photo by Ann Fahl*

Steam

Now the quilt has been forced into its original shape. Using a steam iron or steamer, hover slightly above the quilt top, and the let steam fill the quilt layers. You will see some of the areas that were forced back to position begin to relax and smooth out right before your eyes. Liberally steam the surface several times until it lies flat. Never use the iron or steamer to apply pressure on the quilt because this will flatten the quilting stitches. Let the iron hover ¼˝ to ½˝ above the surface.

Let the quilt cool and dry completely. This could take five minutes to an hour or more, depending on the humidity. Remove all the straight pins on the outside edges. If the quilt is properly blocked, it will just lie there and not snap back out of shape. If it starts to draw up, re-pin, steam again several times, and let it remain pinned overnight.

Trim the Edges

After the pins are removed, trim the outside edges with scissors or a rotary cutter and ruler. Your edges will be arrow-straight, easy to bind, and will look great. If the quilt is bed size, I use a pencil and a ruler to mark the edge. Cut off excess batting and backing with scissors.

Trim edges after final blocking. *Photo by Ann Fahl*

PURPLE-EYED SUSANS, *Ann Fahl © 2008, 16½˝ × 16½˝, wool batting*

Machine Quilting *Basics*

Once the three layers have been basted together, it is finally time to quilt and watch your work begin to come to life! Put on your quilter's gloves, and pick out the thread colors you will be using.

The basting safety pins hold the layers together and secure the straight of the grain. Just as in hand quilting, work from the center out to the edges. Put the quilt under the darning foot, and let's dance!

HOLDING THE QUILT

Smooth the quilt surface with your gloved hands. As you get used to the process, you will find that you are constantly changing the position of your hands as needed. Basically the palms of the hands should be down, flat on the surface of the quilt, with thumbs spread wide in front of the darning foot. Continually smooth the fabrics by gently pushing down and slightly pulling the hands apart. Actually you are smoothing the quilt between the basting pins. Remove basting pins that are in the way of the needle. Never sew over them.

Basic hand position

MANAGING MACHINE SPEED

There is conflicting information on how fast the machine should be stitching while quilting. Some say the machine should go fast, and others say a moderate speed is better. Beginners like to stitch slowly, so what is a quilter to do?

This is what I tell my students: If the lines of stitching look uneven or jerky, you are stitching too slow—speed up your machine. The faster you go, the smoother your stitches will become. Turn up the volume on the music so you develop a rhythm in your work.

Put another way, if you literally can count the number of times the needle goes up and down, you are sewing too slow. Press on the foot pedal a little more. When the stitching evens out, that is the speed you should be quilting. As you come to an outside edge, or have to quilt around a fancy appliqué, go ahead and slow down a little. When you are done with the tricky areas, speed up again. Soon you will develop a rhythm for your quilting style.

STARTING AND STOPPING

When you begin, bring the bobbin thread up to the top. Take several small stitches in one direction, backtrack over them, and then proceed with the design. This is called anchoring the thread. Do this *every* time you begin to quilt.

When you come to the end of an area, do the same thing. Take your last 2 or 3 stitches, sew back over them, and stitch in place a few additional stitches. This will anchor or lock the threads. Try to finish on the outside edge of a shape, in a seam, or where there will be another line of stitching in the same area. If no additional stitching will be done to secure the end, pull your threads to the back, knot them, and hide the ends inside the batting. With a hand-sewing needle (or a self-threading one) pull the ends into the batting, tug on the thread a little to bury the knot, and clip the threads so the ends disappear back inside the quilt.

Before quilting, bring bobbin thread up to top; hold both threads away from needle.

If you have the needle up/down option on your machine, experiment with how you want this set. When I stop, I prefer to have the needle in the down position, but not all the experts agree with this. If the project has been moved or adjusted in some way, the needle might not create the next stitch where you want it. So proceed slowly and learn how you like to use this option.

MANIPULATING THE QUILT UNDER THE MACHINE

The most awkward part of quilting is in the beginning when starting the decorative work in the center. Fold or roll up one or more sides so the center is more accessible. When the edges are folded up, they can't fall off the edge of the table, pull down, and make it difficult to move the quilt around.

As the center is filled up with quilting stitches, the quilting becomes easier. Not only is it easier to access the outside edges of the quilt, but also you have established a rhythm for yourself after you've spent a few hours quilting on your new project. It is no longer necessary to have the quilt all folded up; let it open up as you work.

The beauty of free-motion quilting is that you don't have to pivot and turn the entire quilt to create circles or patterns. Simply move your gloved hands on the quilt surface in a circle, and the stitching will be drawn before your eyes.

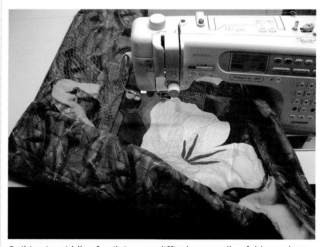

Quilting in middle of quilt is most difficult part; roll or fold up edges to make it easier to work in center. *Photo by Ann Fahl*

> ### Tip
> After you feel comfortable with manipulating the quilt, change the position of the quilt from time to time. This will avoid the designs lining up in the same direction.

ELIMINATING DRAG

The larger the quilt, the more it will drag or resist your efforts to move it. I never took physics in school, but I know what drag is. While dancing with thread on my quilt, I need to make small movements as I create intricate quilt patterns across its surface. To make these movements, it is difficult to move the entire quilt each time you make a scallop, circle, or loop. Push in the outer edges of the quilt toward the needle so you have a pile of quilt behind the needle. This way, just the small area that is being quilted needs to move. It doesn't look pretty, but it works. Please notice in the photo below that I am also wearing the quilt. A medium to large quilt wants to hang over the front edge of the sewing table. This also causes a lot of drag on the quilt. Lift it up, and let it rest on your chest or over your shoulder. You will look lovely.

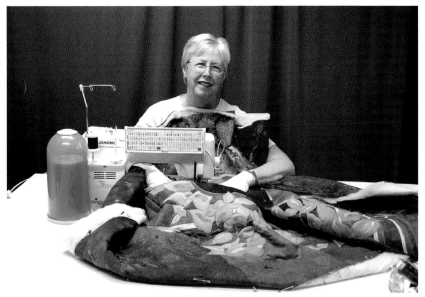

Keep edges of quilt pushed toward area you are quilting. *Photo by Ann Fahl*

TAKING BREAKS

Remember to take frequent breaks from your sewing. Every 20 or 30 minutes you should get up, stretch, move around, do a household task, or take a walk. Think of things to do to break up your sewing sessions. Sewing for long periods of time is tiring for your arms, shoulders, back, and eyes. Breaks allow your body to change its position and rest for a bit.

As much as I hate household chores, they can provide the needed breaks. Things such as pulling food from the freezer for dinner, starting a load of wash, checking the mail, and walking the dog will help you get mundane housework done while giving you a needed change of pace from your sewing machine for a few minutes.

Breaks help keep the quality high, too. If you are getting weary, you will make mistakes and have to rip out stitches.

Don't Forget to *Take Breaks*

Once you get in the groove of machine quilting, it is hard to stop. When you start quilting each day remember to quilt for a little while, then stop and check the backside of the quilt. I've learned the hard way—I'm singing, quilting, and I forget to check. Set a timer for fifteen to twenty minutes. When it rings, flip the quilt over and check your stitches closely. If there is a problem, it's better to know after twenty minutes than after two hours or more! Machine quilting stitches are time-consuming to remove.

The Four Stages *of* Quilting

Quality machine quilting is done in four stages:

Stage 1: Stabilizing the seams

Stage 2: Detailing the design

Stage 3: Creating decorative fill motifs in the empty areas of the quilt

Stage 4: Quilting the border and corners

STAGE 1: STABILIZE THE SEAMS

Before the glamorous part of the quilting can begin, the layers need to be secured. I prefer to use monofilament thread, in the top and the bobbin (page 32), sewn with a 75/11 or 80/12 universal machine needle. Begin by stitching down the center vertical seam, stitching in-the-ditch or exactly in the seamline, from the top of the quilt, down to the lower edge. Repeat this on all the vertical seams. This holds all the layers together securely. Remove the basting safety pins as you get close to them.

The securing is always inside the border. The outside should remain unstabilized until the center is completely quilted.

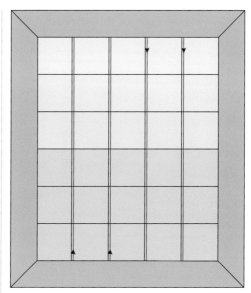

Stitch vertical seams with monofilament. Never stabilize border until center quilting is complete.

Smooth As You Go

As you quilt, smooth the quilt surface between your hands. Smooth between the pins and seams. You will get used to doing this as you move across the surface. Press down with gloved hands, and gently pull your hands apart. You will find that it is necessary for your hands to be moving continuously. The quilt will be smooth and tuck-free on both the top and back. After some practice, this will feel natural to you.

After you finish the vertical seams, stabilize the horizontal seams if needed. Quilts that will get a lot of use and washing will require stabilizing in both directions. Continue until all the quilt blocks have stitching around all sides, with the exception of the border.

As the stabilizing is completed, controlling and smoothing the quilt top gets easier because the sections to smooth with your hands get smaller. To have easier access to the quilt center, roll or fold the unquilted edges. Continue to roll and unroll as you manipulate the central portion of the quilt.

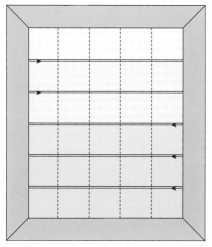

Stabilize horizontal seams if quilt will be heavily used and washed. This step is not necessary on wall quilts.

Note

If there is an appliqué or embellishment covering the seam to be stabilized, stitch around it, and continue along the seam. I prefer not to stop and cut the thread when stitching with monofilament. This will make your task a little easier when you get to the next step of detailing the design.

STAGE 2: DETAIL THE DESIGN

Most of my quilts have a pieced background and an appliquéd or embroidered subject. After the seams have been stabilized, I continue the process. With monofilament thread still in the top and bobbin, I sew around every little flower, petal, and leaf on the quilt. The plan is to sew from the center out to the edges, but in reality, I wander across the surface, sewing around all the small segments, trying not to stop and cut my thread. It's best to keep sewing for as long as you can without stopping. If your quilt is all patchwork, stabilize in and around all the important seams in the blocks.

Why use monofilament? This thread is clear or smoke-colored and cannot be seen. It hides in the seamlines and virtually disappears around appliqué and embroidery. When used in the appropriate way, it can be your friend. Do not listen to those that tell you how bad the thread is. Outlining all your blocks and designs is where monofilament is at its best, so just use it.

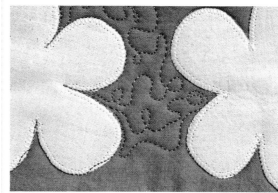

Outlining with monofilament: Flower on right has been outlined in monofilament, and stitching cannot be seen. Flower on left has been outlined with violet quilting thread, and no matter how good you are at quilting, sometimes you will run over edge of appliqué where stitching will be seen.

Now that all the stabilizing work is finished, step back and take a look at your quilt. You may be disappointed at its appearance at this point because it is at the saggy baggy stage. Some parts are quilted, and some not, so the unquilted areas appear droopy.

Coleus leaves have been outlined with monofilament; other areas appear puffy, uncontrolled, and saggy. Once these areas have been quilted, the saggy look will disappear.
Photo by Ann Fahl

Learning to Dance

Once the quilt has been detailed, or stabilized, it is divided into smaller, easier-to-control sections. It is time to begin the dance, one baby step at a time. If you want to be a dancer, you must spend time practicing and perfecting your steps and moves. It takes years to become a prima ballerina, so be patient with yourself. You will find that you will improve every day, and with each project you quilt.

After practicing on a small sample (page 37), it is time to quilt on the actual project!

As I've mentioned, I like decorative thread in the top of my machine and a bobbin thread underneath for dancing. Nothing will enhance your stitching more than a thread that shines. It is a beautiful contrast to the fabrics that most of us use to make quilts. When you have the machine threaded, make a small quilt sandwich with a piece of your batting and a layer of fabric on top and one underneath. *Always test your stitching* for a minute or two on your sample. Check both sides of the sample to make sure that your stitch is balanced, making an adjustment in the tension if necessary (pages 31–33). When everything is set, start quilting in the center of the project and work out to the edges. Quilting to music will help you immensely.

Let's mention the quality of the machine you are using. Personally, I have found that each time I upgrade to a new machine, my stitches and techniques improve a little more too. You can only go as far as your machine will let you. If you have an old clunker machine, you will only be able to dance with heavy clogs. If your machine is easy to use and becomes an extension of your arms, you will be able to dance with beautiful pink slippers that have sparkly ribbons. If you need to upgrade your sewing machine, find the model you want, then ask for it for Christmas, Mother's Day, your birthday, or Valentine's Day, or just go out and buy it.

The more time you spend quilting, the better you become. Experience and improvement is a lifetime journey; you will always get better!

STAGE 3: CREATE DECORATIVE-FILL MOTIFS

Simple quilt motifs are the building blocks of quilting. You will find some motifs to try in Quilting Motifs, pages 66–69. I would suggest that you practice each motif for as long as possible. Create some batting sandwiches that are placemat size or larger, 24″ × 24″, by putting a solid piece of cotton on top and on back of a similarly sized piece of batting. Lower the feed dogs, install a darning foot, a topstitch needle, and some great thread, and begin quilting. Practice until you are sick of the design. Like playing the piano, you must train your brain how the notes must be played, so difficult passages are played over and over again. Practice, and the motif will just emerge from your sewing machine because it is now part of the data stored in your brain. When you feel comfortable with it, include that motif in the next quilt you make.

STAGE 4: QUILT THE BORDER AND CORNERS

Choosing the Border

After the quilt center is filled with stitching, it's time to concentrate on the border. I like to change the darning foot to a closed type. An open-toe foot has a tendency to get caught in the edges and in the batting.

In order to control all the fullness in the outside edges of the border, choose a motif that frequently crosses the outside edge. Borders stitched on the sewing machine that are parallel to the outside edges of a quilt tend to lengthen or stretch out the edges, resulting in wavy and uncontrolled edges.

These quilting motifs tend to stretch edges out of shape.

Motifs that are stitched across the edges in some way help to ease in the fullness of the border and control the outside edges so they lie flat and smooth. Examples of simple, effective borders can be found on page 69.

These quilting motifs cross outer edge, help ease in fullness, and lie flat.

Quilting the Border

When actually quilting the border I find it most comfortable to stitch in a clockwise direction.

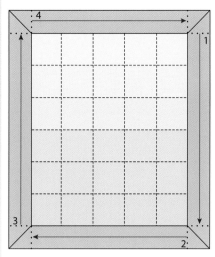

Start at top edge of border #1, gradually work down to bottom, skip corner, and quilt next side.

The border stitching should cover the *entire* border to create a firm edge for the binding. Stitch your motif all the way over the outside edge into the batting before turning around and continuing the border motif. This is why the closed foot is desirable. I like to stitch the motif in a side-to-side motion wherever possible because it is the quickest.

Notice how border is positioned under machine making it easier to use efficient side-to-side motion.

In my experience I've found that it takes almost as long to quilt the border as is does to fill the center. Partly it's because you are anxious to finish, and partly because there are as many square inches to be quilted in the border as there are inside. So stick with it—you will get to the end. For more on border quilting, see page 60.

Corners

The corners may be quilted as you actually turn from one side to the next, or you can wait until you've finished all four sides. It all depends on whether you know what you want to do in the corners. Try to choose something that visually lets the quilting turn the corner. There are a few corner suggestions shown on page 69.

More Thoughts on Quilting

SIGN THE QUILT

Remember to sign your quilt. If you haven't already done this, play with your name and initials, and come up with an idea for including your special mark on every quilt you make. When I took a design class in college, one of our first assignments was to take our initials and make them into a logo. I've used this symbol in my work ever since. Back in grade school, my art teacher said that all artwork should be signed in the lower right-hand corner. I have always done this, and to this day, it doesn't feel right if I sign the quilt in a different location. Feel free to put your signature anywhere.

Signing your work in the quilting not only is your personal mark, but it can also be a security measure. Labels can be removed or torn off, but it takes time to remove a quilted-in signature. Always sign your work—your teacher says so.

AHF signature in lower right-hand corner

QUILTING DENSITY

When you think you've finished all the quilting, pin up the quilt on a wall, and take a critical look. Make note of any areas that appear droopy and need more quilting. I like to turn the quilt over and look at the back, too. Any large unquilted areas need to be filled in with more stitching. The goal should be to have a balanced amount of quilting across the entire surface. If there are large empty spots, go back into those areas and add what is needed.

BEADS AND EMBELLISHMENTS

When I make my quilts, I complete all the embroidery, appliqué, and beading before I baste all the layers together. This hides all the tangles of threads on the back of the quilt top, making a neater quilt back when the quilting is finished.

Since I really enjoy the handwork of beading, I've figured out how to machine quilt around the beads. My students are amazed at how I do it. It isn't really difficult. If you like beads or other enhancements on your quilts, you can try my method.

First, you must be fresh and rested. This is not for the timid or tired quilter. You must have good lighting and be in the mood to concentrate.

1. The darning foot should be the closed-toe type.

2. Use monofilament thread on the top and bobbin.

3. Let the darning foot hop or ride on top of the beads when stitching near them.

4. Stitch slowly and carefully. Remember when I said you shouldn't be able to count the number of times the needle goes up and down when quilting? Forget that piece of wisdom here.

5. When a bead gets stuck on the edge of the foot, just push it down or out of the way with your finger, and proceed. You will figure out that certain angles are better for approaching bugle beads than others. I like to go across the length of the beads, sideways with my darning foot.

6. If you break a bead and the needle is still okay, keep going. Remove the broken bead and put a safety pin in its place.

7. If you have broken more than three beads, it is time to stop for the day, or take a break.

8. When the quilting is finished, go back and replace all the broken beads. Sometimes I don't break any, and then sometimes…

Outline small segments of fused appliqué; note closed-toe darning foot. *Photo by Ann Fahl*

Stitch sideways across bugle bead edge; note monofilament thread does not show at all. *Photo by Ann Fahl*

CHECKLIST FOR QUILTING

Every time you are ready to start quilting a project, go through this list to make sure everything is ready to go.

1. Reduce the machine top pressure on the presser foot to 0.

2. Install a darning foot.

3. Lower the feed dogs.

4. Use a straight-stitch or single-hole throat plate (not all machines have this option).

5. Thread the machine with the presser foot *up*.

6. Make sure the correct size and type of needle is in place.

7. *Always* test your stitch on a sample before quilting on the project. Stitches should be well balanced. They should be slightly rounded on the top and on the underside.

8. Can you see all four corners of the quilt? Make sure they aren't folded under where they may accidentally get caught in the quilting.

Let the *Dancing* Begin

Dancing or quilting levels are designated based on the level of spontaneity or creativity required. First is the ballerina level, then the choreographer, the improvisational dancer, and finally, the jazz dancer as the most free-spirited quilting level. If you are a machine-quilting beginner, you are at the ballerina level. More experienced quilters can work at whatever level they feel comfortable. However, all levels of quilters need to understand their own creative spirit. It's wonderful to dance on your quilt.

The Ballerina:
BEGINNING QUILTING

In ballet classes, children spend hours learning the basic positions. The instructor also works with body and arm positioning to add gracefulness to their basic movement. Like the ballerina, you need to spend a lot of time practicing quilting motifs. You can use just one to fill a whole quilt. You can make baby quilts, small wall pieces, and a lot of placemats or table runners. Try a new motif with each one. Do this again and again. With each new project, choose a different or more challenging design. This is the ballerina level. Practice the basic skills until you feel comfortable and can sew them in your sleep.

For years I sewed nothing but a meandering motif (a large version of stippling) with monofilament thread. Without outside instruction it took a long time for me to progress past this simple motif. At the time, quilters weren't doing too much work with machine quilting, so I literally stumbled through this stage! My only goal was not to have any puckers and pleats on the front or back of my quilts!

Early quilt from 1988 with machine meandering over polyester batting using monofilament thread. The scale is much larger than I use now, but I find the movement and texture over the surface of the triangles to be quite pleasing. *Photo by Ann Fahl*

It was an important day in my life when I discovered decorative rayon thread. I visited a vendor that had a display filled with shiny threads. I went home with a spool of every color she had in that booth. This was the catalyst for my interest in beautiful threads, and my quilting began to improve.

As you would expect, I did a lot of meandering with my wonderful new threads.

When you reach the stage where you are really comfortable with meandering and stippling, it's time to move on to a new stitch. There are thousands of possibilities out there—try them all. Start with some of my favorite motifs, beginning on page 66.

Detail of **INDIANA MEMORIES,** *Ann Fahl © 1995. Photo by Ann Fahl*

Quilted using modified meandering in background with shiny rayon thread; white decorative thread used on swan.

In *My* Opinion…

Meandering and stippling have become very boring to the viewer. This motif has been and continues to be overused because it is a simple motif to learn. Walking through the aisles of any quilt show, you will see far too much stippling on the quilts. This gives a smooth plain look to the areas. As a rule, I like to create more texture and surface interest than stippling provides. Try something else, become more inventive by trying new ideas, and eventually your quilting will become uniquely your own.

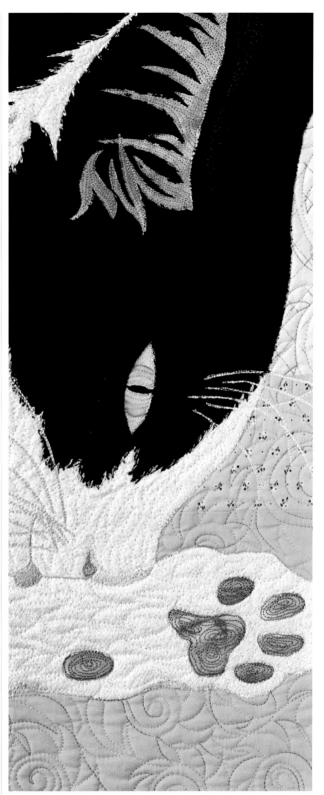

Detail of **MORNING BATH,** *Ann Fahl © 2006, 42˝ × 38˝, wool batting*

Open spiral motif with flame on outer edge provides visually active quilting design.

FISH, FAN AND SPIRAL, *Ann Fahl © 1997, 40½″ × 32″. Photo by Ann Fahl*

Areas between fish are filled with a little clamshell motif. It is easy to make this motif bend or curve around appliqué. It fills empty space quickly. Curves of motif create interesting highlights and shadows. *Photo by Ann Fahl*

As a ballerina, your goal should be to become comfortable with a number of simple quilting motifs beyond simple meandering and stippling. After all, how interesting is a dance with only one step?

> ## If you need *more* quilts to quilt…
>
> Charity quilts are a great way to practice quilting. If you don't have time to make quilt tops yourself, check with a local guild. They often have quilts that need to be quilted.

Practicing Your Skills

It is important to spend time practicing. Fill up a placemat size (18″ × 12″) piece with quilting. Do another and another. Make a quilt using solid colors in 12″ × 12″ squares. Try filling each square with a different motif, and you will have a usable quilt when you are done. The *Dancing Coneflowers* project (page 74) is another way to practice. All of these ideas will give you practice at machine quilting and give you confidence in your abilities. When the motifs become second nature to you, it means you are ready for the next level.

The Choreographer: INTERMEDIATE QUILTING

The choreographer understands the dance and has a complete understanding of the fundamental steps, movements, and variations. Choreographers can create new combinations and new dance steps. When you feel confident as a ballerina and are able to do a number of different motifs with ease, it is time to begin combining motifs. This adds more creativity to quilting and is more fun for you.

Combinations

Create whatever type of dance you'd like. The more combinations you put together, the more flexible you become. Try the following combinations, or make up your own.

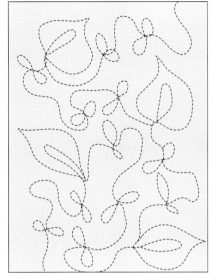

Figure 8 and leaf

Little spiral on string with big closed spiral

Loop and twist with star

Color Dances

Here are some color dances to experiment with. Using variegated thread, stitch one motif every time a certain color appears, and switch to a second motif when another color appears. If you use a variegated thread with a long 20-inch color change, this is fun. Another variation is to change motifs every time the color blue appears. Change motifs after two color changes. You get the idea. Make up your own rules—try whatever is fun yet still challenging your skills.

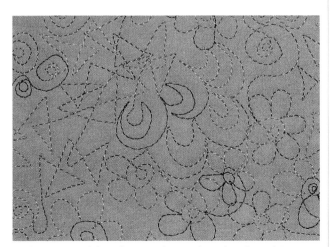

Bright, variegated thread was used to combine closed spiral, ice crystals, seashells, and little flowers. Each motif was stitched during three color changes before switching to next motif. *Photo by Ann Fahl*

Practicing this will make you a more flexible dancer. You will become more and more confident in your skills, and eventually you will find that you can create your own combinations as you quilt.

You can practice some combinations on the *Dancing Coneflowers* project (page 74), or make large samples using combinations of motifs.

As you get bolder, you can change to a new motif whenever the spirit moves you. The more practiced you become, the more motifs you have stored in your brain's data bank; quilting near certain colors and shapes will suggest what needs to be done. When this starts to happen, you know you have become a choreographer!

See what you can put together. It's fun to blend several designs together. Another step in the process would be to experiment with making variations of one design.

Drawing Designs

It can be helpful to draw motifs with pencil and paper first. If you can program your mind with the design, the design will come out of your sewing machine!

Variations

Choose your favorite quilting motif from this book or your notebook, and change it in some way, such as the following:

- Round the edges.

- Add square corners or sharp points.

- Make the loops pointed instead of round.

- Make the loops round instead of oval.

- Echo a simple shape two or three times to enlarge it.

- Add an accent or a new motif.

- Try variegated thread—every time a certain color appears try a new motif.

- Change the scale of the motif: Make it really tiny or really large. Make it larger to emphasize the quilting design, or make it tiny around a design element to make the element stand out.

- Change the thread color.

- Incorporate a written message or your favorite shape.

Placemat filled with variations of spirals

Detail of **HAIRY HOMAGE** (*quilt on page 9*)

Quilting stitch changes in each pictorial unit.

The Improvisational Dancer:
ADVANCED QUILTING

Improvisational dancers take everything they know about their dance specialty and experiment with music and dance to come up with something new and uniquely their own. They are the risk takers, allowing the music to suggest rhythms and movements in their performance. Perhaps what they do in a performance can never be repeated the very same way.

There isn't an artist in this world who can get to this point in her or his development overnight. It takes many hours of working on your skills to become comfortable with improvising in the moment. Loving what you do and wanting to improve are keys for quilters to achieve this advanced level of art. Quilting will become a very personal part of your work as you customize the way you combine your stitches and motifs.

When I reached this level, I found that quilting was totally exhilarating. When I am really in the creative zone and my quilting stitches are flowing, I actually get to a point where I reach what I call a creative high! When an artist or craftsperson is absorbed in a project, the brain starts producing endorphins and can reach a state of euphoria. People who walk, jog, or run have a similar, milder experience. Actors and musicians have this same feeling during and following a live performance. So quilt, go for the creative high—you will feel like you are soaring!

How Do You Begin?

How do you do it? After the top is blocked and the quilt is pin basted and stabilized, you are ready to begin the quilting process. When you're in the groove, you don't need a plan or drawings; you just sit down and begin quilting from the center out to the edges. It is extremely satisfying when everything flows together to create the finished quilt.

However, not all quilts have this wonderful creative flow. Some require more advanced thought and planning. When you come up with an interesting quilt top, make a list of all your thoughts and ideas as you are making it. If you're lucky, you'll also have some quilting ideas while you are piecing and embroidering. Remember that quilting notebook mentioned earlier (page 25)? This is another time that it will come in handy. Flip through all the pages to find ideas.

Dancing on Paper

In *Triangles and Beads II* (at right), the spaces between the beads were so long and narrow that designs I had used in the past just weren't appropriate. I asked my friends for ideas, and one of them suggested using bright variegated thread for the stitching. Then I traced my beading design, full size, on paper and spent several evenings doodling in the narrow curved spaces. Watching TV is a great time for doodling, so is talking on the telephone—part of your brain is occupied with the activity, the other more creative half can just wander around and play on the paper. It might be that just a small part of your doodles will appeal to you. Circle the best part, and save it in your notebook.

*Detail of **TRIANGLES AND BEADS II** (quilt on page 22). Photo by Ann Fahl*

Creating a Plan

It took almost a year for me to put together a plan for all the beaded areas, and I repeated it as I quilted across the patterns. I must admit, it wasn't a year of active planning; it was a year of gathering courage and confidence to quilt inside the strange shapes. I love it now. I love all the colors, the sparkle of the beads, and the many quilting motifs that took so long to bring together. Not all quilts just simply flow from your fingertips and sewing machine. Some actually take a lot of work and planning before they will begin to flow for you. So whether the quilting is planned or just spontaneous, it will still be uniquely yours.

Is this too much planning for you? The above-mentioned advance work and doodling helps create a plan for a challenging quilt. Having a plan helps guide you and gets you started, so your more creative self can emerge. The plan shouldn't be rigid, but it should provide a framework for you to change and embellish upon as you quilt!

Doodling also helped to create the quilting on the following quilts.

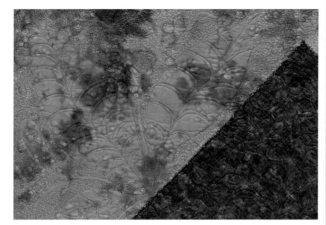

Detail of **TEA PARTY** *(quilt on page 20)*
This corner design was chosen after many trial drawings.
Photo by Ann Fahl

Detail of **TRILLIUM IN THE SUN** *(quilt on page 20)*
After struggling with a more realistic quilting motif, I decided to use a combination of spirals and veins on the leaves. *Photo by Ann Fahl*

Dancing on the Quilt

Now that you have confidence in the number of motifs you can stitch, it is time to put them into a *real* quilt. Remember my favorite method of drawing on photos and doodling (pages 37–38)? When you've found the right combination of ideas, it's time to practice on a test sample using your choice of thread. If you like the way the thread looks and you are comfortable with the motifs or combination, then go ahead and begin on the real quilt. Remember, music will help you keep up a good pace and will keep you interested, too. Sing along as you quilt. On Broadway, the actors sing and dance at the same time. You can too.

Dancing on the Border

After you finish the center of the quilt, you can start on the border. Mark what you need to help guide you, and change the darning foot to a closed style. I like a motif that will combine a motif from the central part of the quilt with the border motif.

When I was making *A Quilter's Menagerie* (page 13), I knew I wanted to use the shape of my spiral roses as part of the border design. Just to test my idea, I actually made a sample the same width as the border. Right away I knew that the spiral I had planned was too large and I didn't like the wavy line edge either. I adjusted my plan and ideas to a smaller spiral, and I'm very pleased with the results. Do whatever you have to do to create an effective border—take photos, draw on paper, or make a sample to help you decide what is best. The border is the frame and the final touch that pulls the entire design together.

Sample of large 6½˝ spiral for border that didn't work

Detail of **A QUILTER'S MENAGERIE** *(quilt on page 13)*
Final border with 4½˝ spiral

The more you dance at this level, the more creative you become with your newly found confidence. Even the borders will become more enjoyable and relaxing. Devote some pages in your notebook to border ideas. This level of quilting may take a while before you feel comfortable and proficient. Keep stitching.

I was at this stage for years, and I was quite happy and content to plan and quilt my work this way. Then the right quilt came along, and I became a more free-spirited quilter. I felt like I had put on those beautiful ballet slippers with the ribbons, and I started to dance. When you feel comfortable with this process, you are ready for the next step. You won't even realize that it is happening.

The Jazz Dancer:
INTUITIVE QUILTING

The jazz dancer moves as the music or the creative spirit directs her or him, creating a one-of-a-kind performance. Let music or your own creative energy direct your hands and the machine to create something new and fresh.

Rather than planning areas with certain types of quilt motifs, just pick the appropriate thread for the top and bobbin, and begin. I always have a basic motif in mind to return to when I don't know what else to do at the moment. I call this my default stitch.

Just follow your inner quilting spirit. Do what the fabric or the images in your quilt tell you to do. Start out with something simple like a string of small spirals. Now add a loop or two until the area is filled or you feel like you want to do something else. When I go around the point of a leaf or petal, I like to do a shell or fan motif at the tip, and see where that takes me. Really crank up the music when you do this—the rhythm will help drive or propel you forward to the next idea. Remember your default stitch. This will help keep you sewing continuously, letting the stitches flow from your arms and machine.

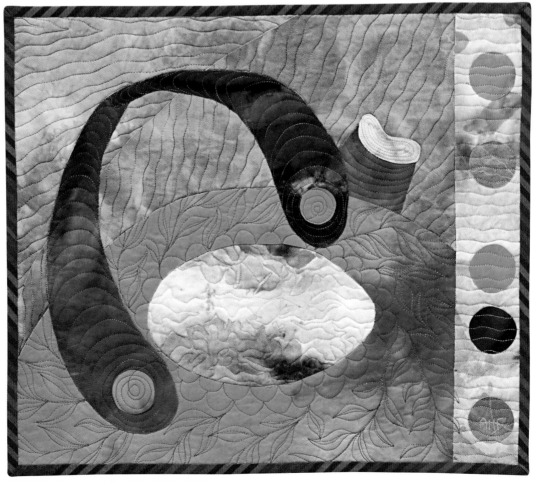

MY TEA KETTLE, *Ann Fahl © 2004, 17½″ × 15½″, wool batting*

Let ideas flow. *Photo by Ann Fahl*

YOUR CREATIVE SPIRIT

On a personal note, an artist must be in the right frame of mind to be creative. You must wait until the time is right to be able to quilt your best. If you have just burned dinner or you are mad at someone, this is not the time to sit down to do your best quilting. Nurture your creative spirit with everything you do in life—this is as important as learning all the skills and techniques you've read about in this book. If you are in the right frame of mind, quilting ideas will flow. This requires a conscious effort on your part, and it is worth the time.

Think of things you can do to lift your mood. I like to wear colorful shoes and socks. Spend less time watching the news. We need to be aware of what is happening in the world, but we don't need to be continually bombarded with news of murder and war. Try to have a positive attitude about life. Surround yourself with creative, positive people. Sew every day. Be organized in your personal life, so you have time for more creative pursuits.

Learn to read your mind and body rhythms, to know when you are able to be creative. This is a process that takes a lifetime, and it's worth reading a book or two on the topic.

After years of sewing and running my own business, I've found that I am most creative in autumn; and I get my best work done in the afternoon. How about you?

When I am quilting this way, I am completely energized as the quilt surface fills up with texture. It is important to note here that not all quilts should be quilted as freely. Some quilts need to be more carefully planned to be successful. If you have that special spark of a feeling about one of your new quilt tops, that is where you should improvise.

Start your improvisational quilting on small quilts. By small, I mean 8 to 12 inches in size, up to about the size of a placemat. Gradually move to larger and larger pieces as your confidence grows. Quilting on your favorite fabric, color, or subject will always seem easier to you. So turn up the music as you are dancing on your quilt. This helps set the mood and tempo of your work. It feels so good.

Something *to* Remember

Even though you are dancing at the highest level, remember all the basics. Test your machine stitching every time you change something (your bobbin or thread color) on your machine. Check the back of the quilt, and block your beautiful new work before attaching the binding.

Detail of **PAINTED GARDEN** *(quilt on page 22)*

Projects

Basic Instructions *and* Quilting Motifs

FUSING, SEWING, AND APPLIQUÉ INSTRUCTIONS FOR ALL PROJECTS

Seams

All seams are ¼˝ and pressed toward one side.

Fusing Shapes

1. When preparing to fuse, trace the shape onto the paper side of the paper-backed fusible web (I prefer Wonder-Under).

2. Cut outside the pencil lines to remove the shape from the larger piece.

3. Press it onto the wrong side of fabric with a *dry* iron.

4. With scissors, cut the shape exactly on the pencil lines.

5. Pull off the paper.

6. Arrange and pin the shapes as directed in the project instructions.

7. Press with *steam* to permanently fuse the shapes into position.

Fusing Stems

I like to fuse a large piece of fabric for stems.

1. Place the requested-size rectangle of fusible web on the wrong side of stem fabric. The length of the stems should be across the grain, from selvage to selvage.

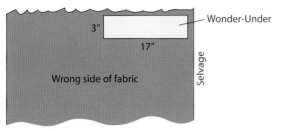

Place length of stems on crosswise grain.

2. Press with a *dry* iron and let cool.

3. Peel off the large piece of backing paper.

4. Use scissors or a rotary cutter to cut the stems using slightly wavy lines.

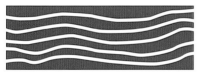

Remove paper backing, and cut curved lines with scissors or rotary cutter.

5. When placed in a project, the strips may be bent and curved almost like bias strips. Pin frequently to hold them in position.

6. Press with *steam* to permanently fuse the stems into position.

Machine Appliqué Process

I prefer to use an open zigzag stitch on the edges of flowers rather than a dense satin stitch. Most are stitched with a stitch length of 0.6 and a width of 2–2.5. This covers the edges well, without creating a heavy line on the outside of each shape.

1. Place a piece of crisp tear-away stabilizer under each fused shape as it is zigzagged into position. This product stabilizes the stitches. Using small pieces makes the project more flexible as you maneuver it under the needle. Using a large piece under the entire project makes it difficult to turn while under construction. Remove the tear-away gently, as the sections are completed.

2. Stitching order: Zigzag the pieces that appear to be on the bottom layer first, working up to the layers that appear to be on the top.

3. Press with *steam* on the right side.

QUILTING MOTIFS

Try each of the quilting motifs on the following pages. They are arranged in order of difficulty. All of them are used in the projects. An arrow indicates the starting point of each one.

QUILTING MOTIFS

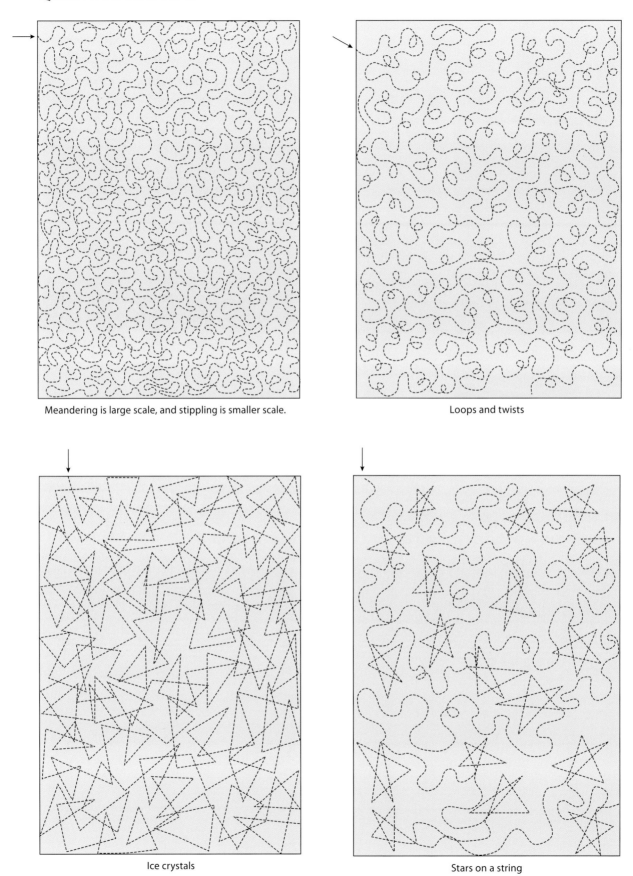

Meandering is large scale, and stippling is smaller scale.

Loops and twists

Ice crystals

Stars on a string

QUILTING MOTIFS

Little clamshells

Seashells, two variations

Closed spirals

Open spirals

QUILTING MOTIFS

Rocks

Leaves and loops

Little flowers

Echoing lines

BORDER IDEAS

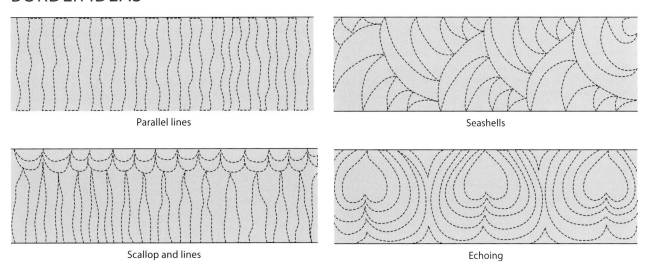

Parallel lines

Seashells

Scallop and lines

Echoing

CORNER SUGGESTIONS

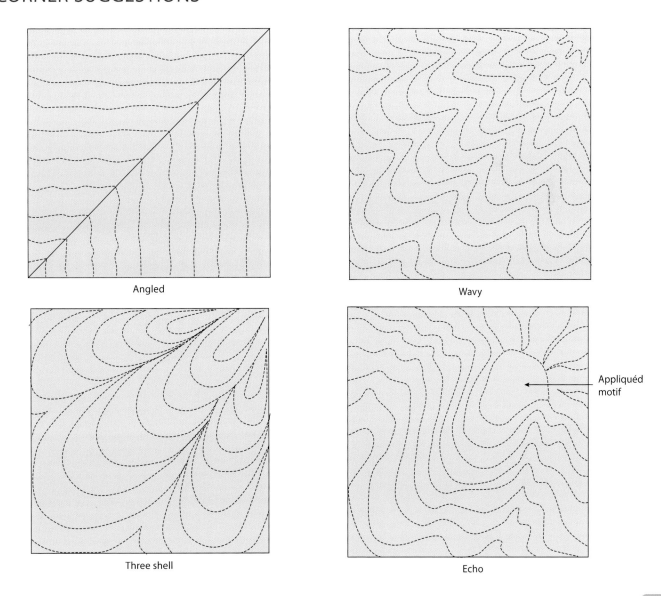

Angled

Wavy

Three shell

Echo

Appliquéd motif

Table Runner Sampler

This table runner is approximately 46″ × 17″ with a cotton blend batting. The sample shown uses a central fabric that changes from dark to light brown with a border of a coordinating stripe. Four easy quilting motifs fill the center. I had fun changing variegated threads as the motifs changed. I used a metallic thread for quilting the border.

MATERIALS AND SUPPLIES

Fabric

- ½ yard for center*
- ½ yard for border
- ⅞ yard for backing
- ½ yard for single-fold bias binding

Requires a usable fabric width of 41″.

Thread

- 40-weight decorative thread (page 28) for quilting
- Bobbin thread (page 32)
- Piecing thread

Other

- Low-loft batting 50″ × 19″

CUTTING

Center fabric

1. Cut a rectangle 41″ × 12″.

2. Fold the fabric lengthwise so it measures 41″ × 6″.

3. Using a pencil, mark a triangle on each end that is 6″ on the end and 5″ from the corner on the top edge. Cut on the marked lines.

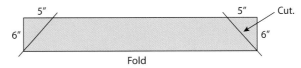

Cut on lines.

Border fabric

1. Cut 4 border strips, each 3″ wide, across the width of the fabric.

2. Trim 2 strips to 3″ × 31″.

3. Cut the remaining 2 strips in half to yield 4 strips 3″ × 20″.

Backing fabric

Cut and/or piece as needed 1 rectangle 51″ × 20″ for the backing.

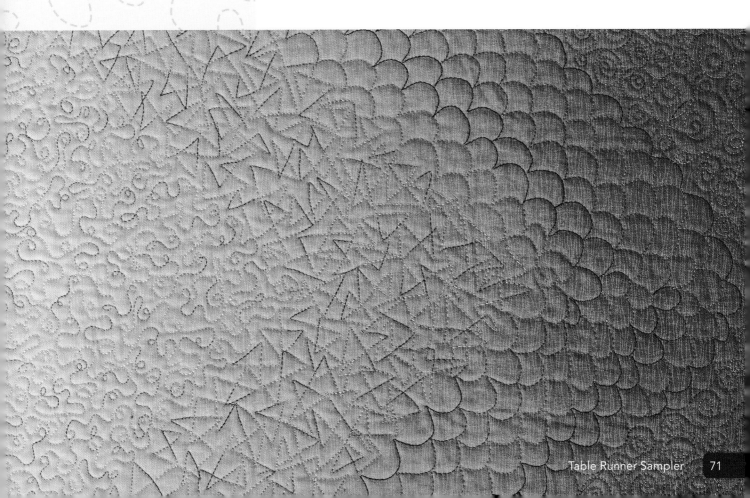

PREPARE THE PROJECT FOR QUILTING

Add the Borders

1. Sew 3″ × 31″ border strips on both long sides. Press.

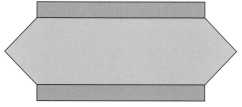

Add side border strips.

2. Sew a 3″ × 20″ strip on one side of pointed edge.

3. Trim off the excess from the long border strip. Press.

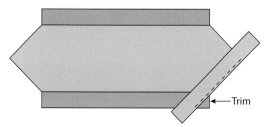

Sew strip on pointed edge.

4. Sew a 3″ × 20″ strip across the adjoining side. Trim. Press.

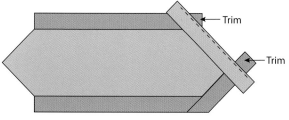

Sew strip on adjoining side.

5. Attach border strips to the opposite end in the same way.

Baste and Mark the Quilt

1. Press the finished top on the right side with steam iron.

2. Layer the quilt back, batting, and top. Pin baste (page 42).

3. With a pencil, mark an 8⅛″ × 8⅛″ square in the exact center of the runner.

4. With a pencil and ruler, lightly mark lines in 5″ increments.

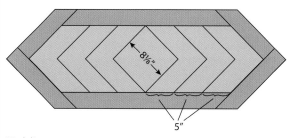

Mark lines.

QUILTING

Quilting Motifs

The quilting motifs used here are simple ones. You may change them to match your quilting skill level.

1. Use the loop and twist motif in the center square.

2. The pencil lines are straight. Quilt the motifs out to the line. When starting the next motif, let the quilting fill any empty spaces on either side of the line so the line is not visible when all the quilting is finished. This way the motifs will blend into one another.

3. Use the ice crystals motif to fill the 5″ section on both sides of the center.

4. Use the little clamshells motif to fill the next section on both sides.

5. Use the closed spirals to fill the remaining space up to the point on both ends.

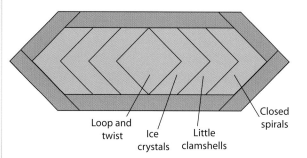

Loop and twist — Ice crystals — Little clamshells — Closed spirals

Pencil lines define sections for quilting motifs. Let motifs blend together. Fill any empty spaces with motif you are using at the time so line isn't obvious.

Quilt the Border

1. The border uses parallel lines; see Quilting the Border (page 51).

2. The sample quilt uses metallic thread in the border. Solid or variegated thread can also be used.

Quilt the Corners

1. As you get close to the outside points, you may mark an angled corner and a square.

Mark areas for angled corner and closed spiral quilting.

2. You can either fill these areas with the angled corner line motif, or you can use one great big closed spiral to fill the space.

FINISHING

1. Trim all the loose threads on top and back.

2. Block the quilted runner (page 44).

3. Trim the edges.

4. Bind the edges.

Dancing Coneflowers

Dancing Coneflowers is approximately 35″ × 53″ with wool batting. This quilt is perfect for practicing basic quilting motifs—it's a Nine Patch quilt with large rectangles instead of squares. For interest, I added coneflowers. If you choose, you can eliminate them, and just practice your machine work on a piece that is actually large enough to be used. Add a border if you'd like to make it larger.

MATERIALS AND SUPPLIES

Fabric

- 9 fat quarters in blues and purples
- 1 fat quarter of white
- 1 fat quarter of green
- 9″ × 9″ square of yellow
- 1¾ yards for backing
- ⅝ yard for single-fold bias binding

Thread

- 40-weight decorative thread (page 28) in white, yellow, and green for stitching the flowers
- 40-weight decorative thread (page 28) for quilting the blocks
- Bobbin thread for all colors (page 32)
- Monofilament thread (page 32)
- Piecing thread

Other

- 1 yard paper-backed fusible web, 17″ wide
- Batting 39″ × 57″
- 2 yards crisp tear-away stabilizer, 20″ wide

CUTTING

Blue and purple fabrics
Cut 9 rectangles 12″ × 18″ for the background.

Green fabric
Cut 1 rectangle 7″ × 15″ for the stems.

Backing fabric
Cut and/or piece as needed 1 rectangle 40″ × 58″ for the backing.

PREPARE THE PROJECT FOR QUILTING

Make the Background

1. Arrange the blue and purple rectangles in a manner that pleases you.

2. Sew the rectangles together in 3 rows of 3, and press.

3. Sew the 3 rows together, and press.

4. Prepare the 7″ × 15″ fabric for the stems with paper-backed fusible web (page 65).

5. Cut 9 narrow strips from the fused green fabric, each about ¼″ wide by 15″ long.

6. Trace, fuse, and cut 9 flowers and 9 centers (patterns are on page 78).

7. Place the flowers, centers, and stems on the quilt top. The narrow strips can be gently curved with your fingers and pinned frequently into position.

8. Press all the pieces into position using the *steam* setting on the iron.

9. Appliqué or embroider the flowers in place (page 65).

10. Block the top (page 40).

Baste and Secure the Quilt

1. Using a pencil, mark a line 4″ in from the outside edge on all four sides for a quilted border.

2. Layer, and pin baste (page 42).

3. Quilt in the seams with monofilament to stabilize them (page 48).

4. Outline the flowers and stems with monofilament (page 49).

QUILTING

With the seams secured with monofilament thread, you are ready for the decorative quilting. I've listed the motifs both in order of difficulty and in the order they should be sewn. The area numbers correspond to the Quilting Placement Diagram (page 77). For a review of the quilting motifs, refer to pages 66–68.

- **Area 1:** Meandering motif in the lower corner of center block: This small amount should help to warm up your quilting skills.

- **Area 2:** Loops and twists: You may stop the stitch when you reach a seam, or you may let it run over into the next rectangle to gradually blend your quilting motifs together.

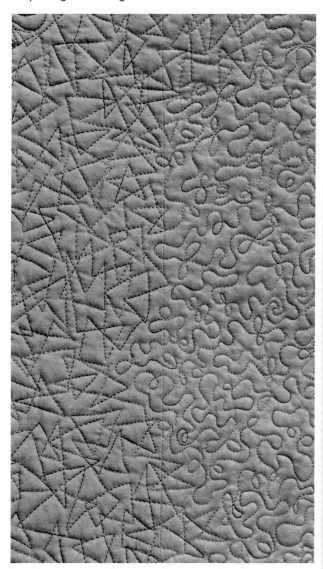

Let quilting cross seamlines so motifs appear to blend.

- **Area 3:** Ice crystals: Move slowly and deliberately to get short, straight lines. Start by drawing a 5-pointed star, but never quite finish the star. Just keep moving and create overlapping triangle-like shapes.

- **Area 4:** Stars on a string: Attach the stars together with some loops and a twist.

- **Area 5:** Spirals: Fill them from the inside out or the outside in. Your choice.

- **Area 6:** Clamshells: Great to fill an area fast. I start at the bottom and move up. It is more interesting when it is curved or stitched on an angle.

- **Area 7:** Seashells: Change the number of times you go around the first little loop, and change the size to add some interest.

- **Area 8:** Echoing: This one has been a part of quilting forever. Straight lines aren't interesting, so add some curves and change the distance between the lines of stitching.

- **Area 9:** Open spirals: Similar to #5 spiral above. When you stitch the spiral into the center, be sure to allow enough room to exit the spiral without touching the other stitching lines.

- **Area 10:** Rocks: One of my personal favorites. Go around each circle two times, and vary the sizes of the circles. This takes more time than the rest of the motifs, but the appearance is worth it.

- **Area 11:** Leaves and loops: First create the leaf shape, and then the inside loop. Link the leaves together with a loop and twist.

- **Area 12:** Little flowers: This is a fun motif. Begin with a little spiral in the center, and create scallops around it for the petals. Link the flower shapes together with a loop and twist.

Quilt the Border

This is the easiest part, because the border is so accessible. Change your open-toe darning foot to a closed-toe style. Remember to stitch in a side-to-side direction wherever possible. Sometimes you will find little bubbles of excess quilt top. Remove the safety pins, smooth the bubble out to the edge, and then re-pin. (For a review of the following motifs, refer to page 69.)

- **Area 13:** Parallel lines: Stitch from inside the first corner to inside the next. This motif fills up the border fast. Leave the corner empty.

- **Area 14:** Scallops and lines: Create one row of scallops, then go back up the side, echoing with the next row of scallops. Then add the wavy parallel lines on the way back down the side.

- **Area 15:** Seashells: Just like the quilting motif, but make it a little larger and more open. Stitch one direction along the inside edge of the border, then go back down, filling up the empty spaces on the outside edge.

- **Area 16:** Hearts: Using a pencil, evenly space 5 small 2″ hearts. On an end of the border, quilt a heart, then echo it several times. Move on to the next heart and repeat. Go back and fill any remaining empty spaces on the outer edge.

Quilt the Corners

You are almost done. The corners will go quickly because they are so small. You are anxious to finish the quilt, but you must take time to quilt the corners so the quilting looks like it flows from one side to the next. Mark if necessary. (Refer to page 69 for a review of the following motifs.)

- **Area 17:** Angled corner.

- **Area 18:** Echo the shape of the coneflower: You can echo *any* shape you desire.

- **Area 19:** 3-lobed seashell: Then echo it out to the edge.

- **Area 20:** Wavy lines: And echo them.

FINISHING

1. Trim all the loose threads on top and back.

2. Block the quilt (page 44).

3. Trim the edges.

4. Bind the edges.

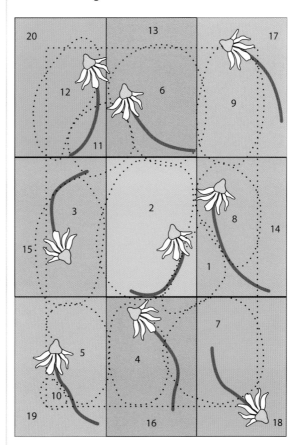

Quilting Placement Diagram
Feel free to add your own ideas.

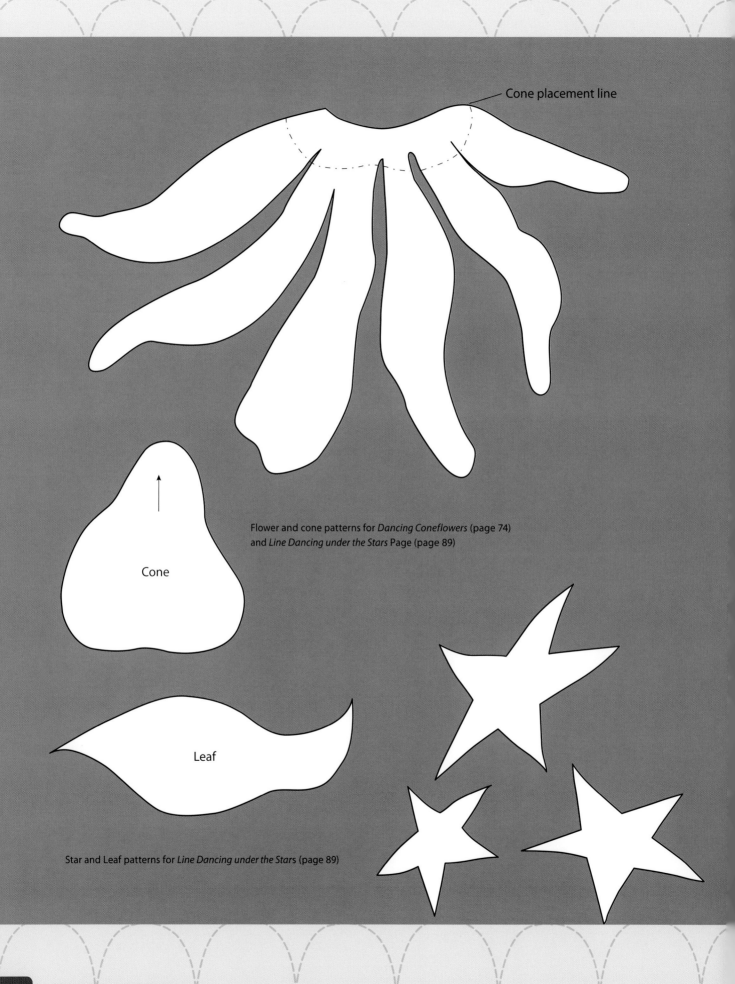

Cone placement line

Cone

Leaf

Flower and cone patterns for *Dancing Coneflowers* (page 74) and *Line Dancing under the Stars* Page (page 89)

Star and Leaf patterns for *Line Dancing under the Stars* (page 89)

This little quilt is approximately 28″ × 32″ with wool batting. These dancing tulips will help you loosen up your quilting style simply by following the print in the background and will help you feel comfortable quilting in all directions. You will see how easy and fun it can be without marking anything. You need to choose a print for the background that is subtle in coloration, yet has a printed element that you can follow such as flowers, circles, paisley, and so on.

Dancing in the Wind

MATERIALS AND SUPPLIES

For this project's background, I chose a pink and rose allover classic paisley pattern. I used 3 different red fabrics for the tulips, and 3 green fabrics for the stems and leaves: dark for leaves, medium for stems, and light for leaves in the foreground. The background fabric and green fabrics are strip-pieced to create a simple border.

Fabric

- 1 yard pink
- ⅓ yard light green
- ⅓ yard dark green
- 1 fat quarter medium green
- 8″ × 7″ rectangle tulip red 1
- 12″ × 8″ rectangle tulip red 2
- 12″ × 8″ rectangle tulip red 3
- 1 yard for backing
- ⅝ yard for single-fold bias binding

Thread

- 40-weight thread (page 28) for appliqué in red for tulip, light and dark green for leaves, medium green for stems
- 40-weight decorative thread (page 28) in pink for quilting
- Bobbin thread in blending colors (page 32)
- Monofilament thread (page 32)
- Piecing thread

Other

- 1 yard crisp tear-away stabilizer, 20″ wide (page 65)

- 2 yards paper-backed fusible web, 17″ wide
- Batting 31″ × 35″

CUTTING

Pink fabric

Cut 1 rectangle 23″ × 26″ for the background.

Cut 4 strips 2″ × 42″ for the border.

Cut 2 rectangles 2″ × 3″ for the side borders.

Light green fabric

Cut 1 square 3″ × 3″ for a border corner.

Cut 1 rectangle 3″ × 4″ for a border corner.

Cut 2 strips 2″ × 42″ for the border.

Dark green fabric

Cut 1 square 3″ × 3″ for a border corner.

Cut 1 rectangle 3″ × 4″ for a border corner.

Cut 2 strips 2″ × 42″ for the border.

Medium green fabric

Cut 1 rectangle 3″ × 17″ for the stems.

Backing fabric

Cut and/or piece as needed 1 rectangle 32″ × 36″ for the quilt backing.

PREPARE THE PROJECT FOR APPLIQUÉ AND QUILTING

1. Sew together the 2″ × 42″ strips in this order: pink, dark green, pink, light green, pink, dark green, pink, light green, for a total of 8 strips. Press the seams in one direction. Trim 1 edge so that it is straight.

2. Cut the pieced unit into 6 segments each 3″ wide to create the side and top borders, and 2 segments each 4″ wide for the bottom border.

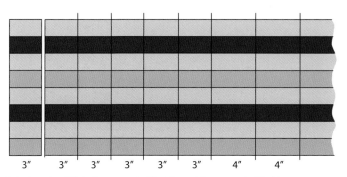

Cut pieced unit into 6 segments 3″ wide and 2 segments 4″ wide.

3. Sew 2 of the 3″ segments together to create the right border. Add a 2″ × 3″ pink rectangle to the light green end. Do the same for the left border.

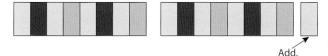

Add.

Sew 2 segments together and add pink rectangle.

4. Sew the border strips to the left and right sides of the quilt. Refer to the photo on page 79 for placement of light and dark green segments. Press seams away from the center.

5. Sew the 2 remaining 3″ segments together to create the top border. Remove the light green rectangle from the end.

Remove.

Sew 2 segments together and remove light green rectangle.

6. Sew a 3″ × 3″ square (1 light and 1 dark) on both ends of the top border.

7. Attach the top border, using pins where the seams meet at the corners. Refer to the photo on page 79 for placement of light and dark green segments. Press seams away from the center.

Note: The bottom border is made from 4″-wide segments, so it is wider than the other 3 sides.

8. Sew together the 2 segments that are 4″ wide for the bottom border.

9. Sew a 3″ × 4″ rectangle (1 light and 1 dark) on both ends of the bottom border.

10. Attach the bottom border, using pins where the seams meet at the corners. Refer to the photo on page 79 for placement of the light and dark green segments. Press seams away from the center.

APPLIQUÉ

Prepare the Appliqué

Trace and fuse the red and green fabrics, using the patterns on pages 83–84:

Red 1: 1 medium tulip and 1 small tulip

Red 2: 1 large tulip and 1 medium tulip

Red 3: 1 large tulip, 1 medium tulip, and 1 small tulip

Light green: 4 leaves: 2 leaves as drawn, 1 leaf 1″ longer, 1 leaf 2″ shorter

Dark green: 2 leaves

Use a piece of paper-backed fusible web 3″ × 17″ and medium green fabric to create ⅜″-wide stems (page 65).

Place the Appliqué

I prefer to place the paper-backed pieces onto the background and move them around until I am happy, and then remove the paper, pin in place, and steam press to fuse into position.

1. Place the 6 tulip leaves on the lower edge of the background as in the project photo (page 79).

2. Place tulips above the leaves.

3. Place stems between the flowers and the leaves. Bend and curve them (page 65).

4. Tuck the top end of each stem under a flower. The lower end can be tucked under a leaf or cut off at the lower edge of the quilt top.

5. Press using a steam setting, removing pins as you get close to them.

Machine Appliqué

1. Place a piece of tear-away stabilizer under each shape as it is zigzagged into position.

2. Zigzag the leaves behind the stems first, and then the stems, the top leaves, and the flowers (page 65).

3. Remove the tear-away stabilizer. Press.

4. Block the fused and appliquéd top (page 40).

Baste and Secure the Quilt

1. Layer and pin baste (page 42).

2. Outline the flowers, stems, and leaves with monofilament (page 49):

Note: Test your machine stitches first on a scrap.

Begin outlining the center tulip flower, and then go down the stem, back up another stem, around the flower, down the stem around a portion of a leaf, up the next stem, and so on.

The general path of outlining the shapes is from the center out. With this design it's from the center to the right half, then from the center to the left half. Remember to leave the border unsecured.

QUILTING

Quilt the Center

1. Change to a decorative shiny thread on the top and a blending bobbin thread. The quilt in the photo uses a pink variegated thread on top and a rose bobbin thread. Test the stitching of the newly installed thread.

2. Following the pattern of the fabric, quilt from the middle tulip up, and then the tulip below. Pay attention to your hand position, always gently smoothing and lightly pulling the fabric layers.

3. Completely quilt the background surrounding the tulips.

4. Quilt some detail into the tulips. At the very minimum, follow the petal lines with red thread on top and red in the bobbin.

Add detail quilting on flowers and leaves.

5. Quilt some veins in the leaves with matching green thread.

Note: The border will be looking very uncontrolled at this point. Don't worry.

Quilt the Border

1. Begin at the upper right corner, and quilt the border in a side-to-side motion using the wavy parallel line border quilting motif (page 69). Remember to quilt out into the batting before turning around and stitching back onto the border. Use a closed-toe darning foot.

2. Angled corner stitching works well to finish all four corners.

FINISHING

1. Trim all the loose threads on top and back.

2. Block the quilt (page 44).

3. Trim the edges.

4. Bind the edges.

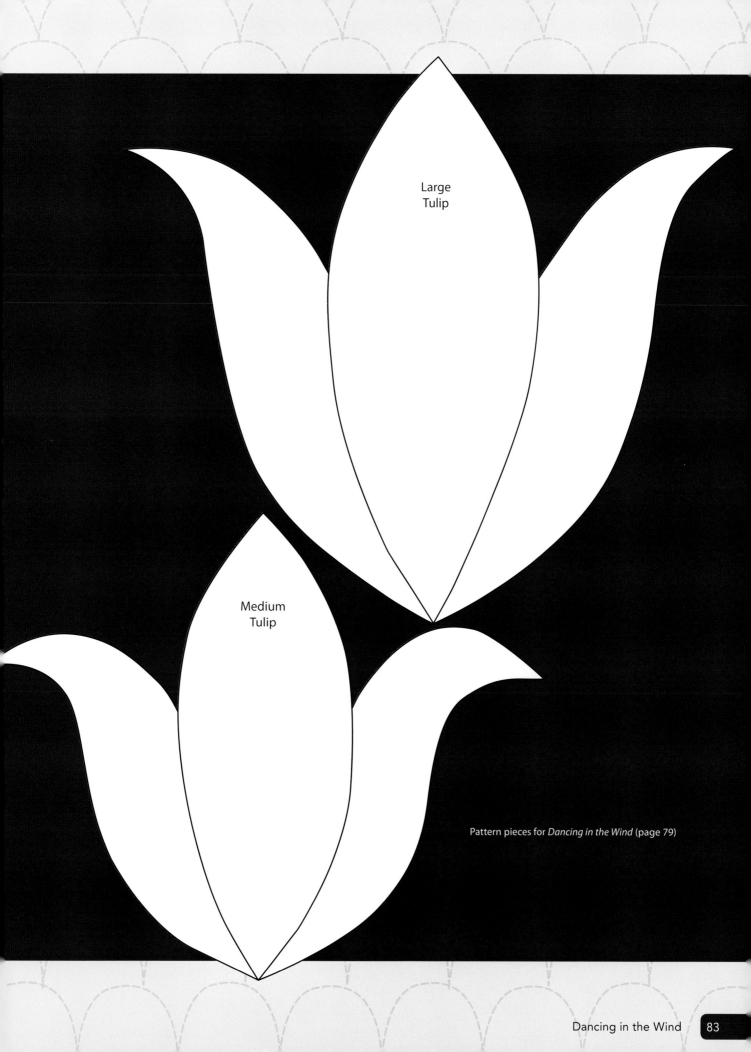

Large
Tulip

Medium
Tulip

Pattern pieces for *Dancing in the Wind* (page 79)

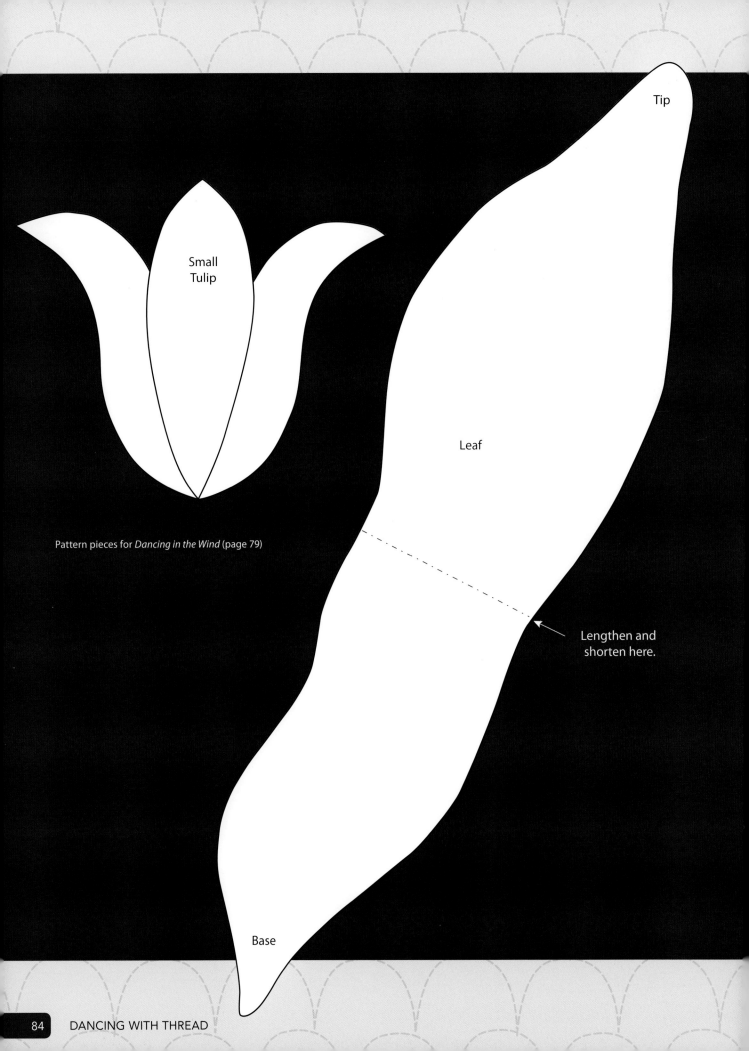

Small
Tulip

Tip

Leaf

Lengthen and
shorten here.

Base

Tip

Pattern pieces for *Dancing in the Wind* (page 79)

Square Dancing

This geometric quilt is approximately 22″ × 33″, with wool batting. It is fused together rather than machine-pieced. It's fun to arrange large blocks of color and fill them up with some interesting quilting. It uses 6″ × 6″ and 12″ × 12″ squares. Give it a try.

MATERIALS AND SUPPLIES

For this project I used medium mottled fabric of blue, turquoise, and blue-violet. There are 2 prints that are light blue, 1 slightly darker than the other.

Fabric
- ½ yard each of 3 mediums: blue, turquoise, and blue-violet
- ½ yard each of 2 light blues
- 1 yard backing
- ⅝ yard for single-fold bias binding

Thread
- 40-weight decorative thread (page 28) for quilting
- Bobbin thread in blending color (page 32)
- Monofilament thread (page 32)

Other
- 1 piece 22½″ × 33½″ of light-weight non-woven iron-on interfacing
- 2 yards paper-backed fusible web, 17″ wide
- UHU glue stick
- Batting 25″ × 36″

CUTTING

Fusible web
On the paper side of the fusible web, draw 3 squares 12″ × 12″, 15 squares 6″ × 6″, and 1 square 3″ × 3″.

Medium blue, turquoise, and blue-violet fabrics
Cut out and press 2 of the 12″ × 12″ fusible web squares onto the wrong side of both the turquoise and the blue-violet fabrics.

Cut out and press 3 of the 6″ × 6″ fusible web squares on the wrong side of each of the 3 medium fabrics.

Light blue fabric
Cut out and press the remaining 12″ × 12″ fusible web square onto the wrong side of a light blue fabric.

Cut out and press 3 of the 6″ × 6″ fusible web squares onto the wrong side of each of the 2 light blue fabrics.

Cut out and press the 3″ × 3″ fusible web square on the wrong side of a light blue fabric.

Backing fabric
Cut and/or piece as needed 1 rectangle 26″ × 37″.

PREPARE THE PROJECT FOR QUILTING

Make the Background

1. Place the non-woven interfacing *fusible side up*. It is best to pin it onto a design wall for better visibility. The non-woven fusible interfacing acts as both a stabilizer and a fusible product.

2. Each square should slightly overlap another by about ½″.

3. Put the 3 large squares onto the fusible side of the interfacing.

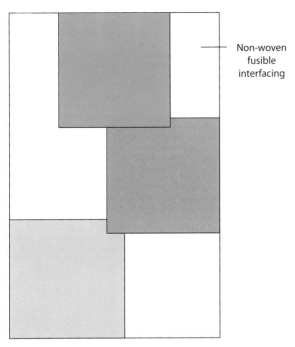

Place 3 large 12″ squares.

4. As you place the remaining squares, remember that there should be a minimum of ½″ overlap of the pieces. Fabric can also hang over the outside edge as well. This will ensure that the interfacing underneath does not show.

5. Place 5 of the light and 1 of the medium 6″ squares as shown in diagram.

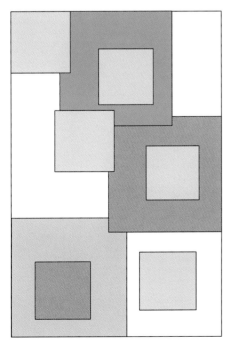

Place 5 of the 6″ squares.

6. The remaining 6″ squares should be tucked underneath to fill in all the empty spaces. I cut several of the squares in half, to create 3″ × 6″ rectangles where an entire square wasn't needed.

7. It may be necessary to cut an extra strip or square to cover an empty spot.

8. None of the interfacing should be visible now. Add an additional light rectangle and the 3″ square for visual contrast.

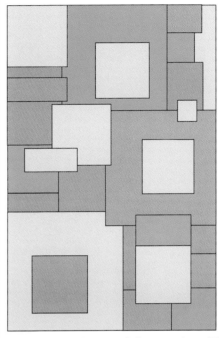

Place remaining 6″ squares, light rectangle, and 3″ square.

9. When you are satisfied with the arrangement of the pieces, press using *a lot of steam*.

10. If there are areas that don't stick, use a glue stick to keep the edges down.

11. Block the fused quilt top (page 40).

Baste and Secure the Quilt

1. Pin baste the layers (page 42). Place extra pins where the fused edges want to curl up.

2. Secure the quilt by stitching 1 or 2 times following the outside edges of the fused squares.

QUILTING

Quilting Diagram

There are only 3 motifs: wavy lines, seashells, and spirals.

1. Quilt using the designs of your choice, or follow my designs.

2. The closed spiral is the focal point of the quilting. I marked 3″–4″ circles with pencil to make sure the outside of each was round.

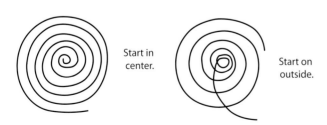

Start in center.

Start on outside.

Closed spiral can be stitched from outside in or inside out.

3. When stitching a spiral from the outside in, it isn't necessary to break the thread to start a new spiral. When ready, travel across the spiral to the place where you will be quilting next. Try to quilt a curved line instead of a straight one.

4. Start with the 4″ spiral near the center of the quilt. Secure the thread in the center, and begin circling the center until you reach the outside edge, then change to the seashell motif. Working from the center spiral to the outside edges, I tried to aim the big loop of the seashell motif away from the center.

5. When you are near one of the 6″ squares, fill them with parallel wavy lines, changing direction each time you start a new square. Make sure that you completely fill the squares with the wavy lines. The stitching line should go all the way to the edge of the block before turning around in-the-ditch and going back in the opposite direction until the block is quilted. This will keep the edges from curling up.

6. Continue to create the seashell motif. Fill in the spirals as marked. Quilt until the surface is full. Feel free to change motifs as the spirit moves you.

7. Quilt the outside edges in a motif of your choice. I used the loops and twists along with parallel wavy lines.

FINISHING

1. Trim all the loose threads on top and back.

2. Block the quilt (page 44).

3. Trim the edges.

4. Bind the edges.

Line Dancing under the Stars is approximately 33″ × 22″ with bamboo batting. This light-hearted quilt has no border, so the cone-flowers and stars can dance as they please. The flowers and stars may be machine appli-quéd or embroidered as desired.

Line Dancing under the Stars

MATERIALS AND SUPPLIES

The background consists of 24 squares. An optional timesaving idea would be to use an ombré fabric, and cut it 33˝ × 22˝.

Fabric

- 30 squares 6˝ × 6˝ in colors ranging from purple to red

- 1 fat quarter of pink

- ¼ yard or 1 fat quarter lighter green

- 1 scrap (6˝ × 8˝) darker green

- 1 scrap (6˝ × 6˝) yellow-gold

- 1 scrap (9˝ × 9˝) pale yellow

- 1 scrap (3˝ × 7˝) light blue

- 1 yard for backing

- ⅝ yard for single-fold bias binding

Thread

- 40-weight decorative thread (page 28) in pink, green, yellow, and light blue for appliqué

- 40-weight decorative thread for quilting

- Bobbin thread in blending colors (page 32)

- Monofilament thread (page 32)

- Piecing thread

Other

- 1 yard crisp tear-away stabilizer, 20˝ wide

- 1 yard paper-backed fusible web, 17˝ wide

- Batting 35˝ × 25˝

CUTTING

Lighter green

Cut 1 rectangle 3˝ × 15˝ for stems.

Backing fabric

Cut and/or piece as needed 1 rectangle 37˝ × 26˝.

PREPARE THE PROJECT FOR QUILTING

Make the Background

1. Arrange the 6˝ squares so that they are 6 across and 4 down. You won't use all the squares you have, but the extra squares give you more design options.

2. The project quilt has 6 purple squares on the top row and 6 red squares on the bottom row. The middle 2 rows blend from purple to red. Move the squares around until the colors change as subtly from purple to red as possible. Look through a reducing glass or a digital camera to get a distance view.

3. Sew the squares together in 4 rows of 6, pressing the seams toward one direction and alternating direction from row to row.

4. Sew the rows together, pressing the seams one way.

Prepare the Appliqué

Appliqué patterns are on page 78.

1. Trace, fuse, and cut 5 flowers from the pink fabric, reversing 2 of them. When cutting, add some variation to the petals by making some wider, longer, or thinner.

2. Trace, fuse, and cut 5 cones from the yellow-gold fabric, reversing 2 of them. Make some of the cones shorter for variation.

3. Fuse a piece of paper-backed fusible web 3″ × 15″ onto the back of the lighter green fabric. Cut 5 stems about ¼″ wide (page 65).

4. Trace, fuse, and cut 5 leaves in each green fabric for a total of 10 leaves.

5. Trace, fuse, and cut 6 pale yellow stars and 3 light blue stars.

Place the Appliqué

Use the photo of the finished quilt (page 89) to help with placement of the pieces.

1. Place the pink flowers so they sit on the second row of background squares. Each flower should straddle a vertical seam.

2. Place the cones in the center of the flowers.

3. Place the stems beneath the flowers, and let them curve down to the bottom edge of the red row of squares.

4. Place the leaves with the darker leaf on the left side and the lighter leaf on the right side of the stem. Stagger their placement so that they appear to be dancing.

5. Place the yellow stars above the flowers. Rotate the stars so that each sits on a different point.

6. Place the blue stars between the flowers.

7. When pleased with the arrangement, peel off the paper backing, and press with steam.

Appliqué

1. Using matching or blending thread, machine appliqué all of the pieces into position. Remember to place a layer of tear-away stabilizer underneath for neater stitches for appliqué (page 65).

2. Block the quilt top (page 40).

Baste and Secure the Quilt

1. Layer and pin baste (page 43).

2. Quilt in the seams with monofilament to stabilize them (page 48).

3. Outline the flowers, leaves, stems, and stars with monofilament (page 49).

QUILTING

1. Just as the flowers are dancing, I want you to try to dance on this one. Think about all the hints I have given you and what you've learned while reading this book. Take a picture of your quilt top, and try out all your ideas first with a pen on paper. This is your final exam!

2. Dance using your own ideas on this delightful quilt.

3. In my quilting I wrote the word *dance* on one side and *dance feel free* on the other side.

FINISHING

1. Trim all the loose threads on top and back.

2. Block the quilt (page 44).

3. Trim the edges.

4. Bind the edges.

5. Be proud of your work: Remember to sign and label the quilt.

Congratulations!
You have successfully completed my dancing program.

Quilting Problem Solving

PROBLEM	SOLUTION
Thread breaks	Check spool to see if thread is wrapped around pin or caught on rough edge of spool.
	Rethread machine.
	Loosen top tension.
	Use next larger size needle.
	Select topstitch or embroidery-type needle.
	Try new needle.
	Skip last thread guide above needle.
	Try stitching more slowly.
	Change position of spool to vertical or horizontal.
Thread tangles	Rethread machine.
	Turn spool around.
	Check position of top spool. Straight-wound spools should sit on vertical pin. Cross-wound spools should sit horizontally or on thread stand.
	Use thread net for small and large cones that are cross-wound.
Needle breaks	Check spool or cone. Thread may have wrapped around vertical pin. Rethread machine.
	Use thread net on cross-wound cones.
	Spool may be overspinning, and thread is wrapping around pin. Use spool cap, felt pad, thread stand, or thread net.
	Check machine manual for how to thread machine. You may be missing something.
	There may be too many thicknesses to stitch through. Avoid quilting in problem area, if possible.
	Replace needle with a larger size.
Irregular loops or tangles on underside	Always thread machine with presser foot in *up* position.
	Remove top thread and bobbin completely, and rethread machine. Thread is not properly seated in tension disks.
	There may be a burr in bobbin case. Take machine in for servicing.
Birds' nests on the back	Pay attention to how long you quilt in one spot. When changing directions, take a stitch or two before moving in new direction. Any more than this will create a little lump of stitches on quilt back.
	If top thread is much heavier than bobbin thread, direction changes in quilting will be obvious, creating small bird's nest. Try using bobbin thread that is one size larger. If using monofilament in bobbin, try 60-weight bobbin thread. If using bobbin thread, try 50-weight thread instead.
	Use bobbin thread that matches or blends with top color.

PROBLEM	SOLUTION
Bobbin thread showing on top	Rethread machine.
	Loosen top tension.
	Remove bobbin from machine, and then put it back into bobbin case.
	Bernina machines: Put bobbin thread through hole in arm of bobbin case.
	Other brands: Tighten bobbin tension (pages 32–33).
	Make sure bobbin thread color matches or blends with top thread.
	Try different type of bobbin thread.
	Use new bobbin.
Top thread showing on back	Rethread the machine, making sure presser foot is *up*.
	Gradually tighten top tension.
	Choose bobbin thread that matches or blends with top thread.
	Try finer bobbin thread.
	If you've tried all the above with no improvement, there may be a burr in bobbin case. Have machine serviced.
Top thread pulling with poorly defined stitches	Try moving quilt a little slower under the needle. This happens especially when doing circles and curves.
	On curves, try speeding up the machine a little bit.
	If this is consistently a problem, tighten the bobbin tension.
Quilt dragging or resisting while sewing	Reduce top pressure on the presser foot to 0. Check machine manual for location of pressure knob. Not all machines have this option.
	Check position of quilt. If hanging over edge of table, it is pulling against you. Push, rather than fold or roll, all parts of quilt closer to needle, so it drags less (page 47).
	If part of quilt is resting in your lap, you have to pull and guide it for stitching. Lift quilt up, and let it rest on your shoulders or chest (page 47).
	On very humid days, it is harder to move quilt on some flat surfaces. Turn on air conditioner or dehumidifier.
	Use SewSlip to make it easier to move and manipulate entire quilt on sewing surface (page 26).
	Some generic darning feet need to be adjusted slightly. Remove foot from machine. Locate bar on attachment that rests above needle screw on machine. Bend it down a little closer to foot. This is not manufacturer recommended, but it works.
	Is there a cat sitting on your quilt?

PROBLEM	SOLUTION
Uneven stitches	Increase speed of machine. This will smooth out stitches. Turn on your favorite music to help you maintain constant sewing speed. Check position of quilt. Any parts hanging over sewing surface will make it difficult to stitch evenly. Push farthest edges toward needle, and let quilt rest on your chest or shoulders (page 47).
Skipped stitches	Rethread machine, making sure presser foot is *up*. Stitch more slowly. Replace needle. Try silicone product on top thread.
Needle catching and snagging	Throw away needle, and put in new topstitch needle. Even if needle is brand new, it's not worth snagging fabric. Always replace needle after 6–8 hours of sewing.
Something wrong in the bobbin	Is your bobbin almost empty? Replace with full one. Completely remove bobbin case from machine, and then reinstall. Are you using a prefilled bobbin? Use bobbin provided by machine manufacturer. Wind thread of prefilled one onto manufacturer-supplied bobbin.
Darning foot squeaks or chirps	Wipe off lint on vertical bar, and lubricate with a dot of Sewers Aid. Darning feet do wear out. Once you've cleaned and lubricated spring area several times, it is time to get a new foot!
Nothing seems to work right on the machine	Turn off power for 10 seconds to let computer reset itself. Check power supply. If you are using power strip or surge protector, plug machine directly into wall outlet. Replace fuse in power strip. Replace power strip. Rethread machine, making sure presser foot is *up*. Take out bobbin, and make sure it is not in backward and unwinding wrong way. Take machine in for servicing. Include sample of problem stitches. Give up for the day. Have a cup of tea and a cookie.

About *the* Author

Photo by Ann Fahl

Ann Fahl lives in Racine, Wisconsin, where she works in her home studio. Her mother always said Ann was born with a crayon in her hand. The family would wake up in the morning to find little Ann standing near the desk, coloring on a piece of paper. In grade school she also spent hours painting with watercolors and practicing origami. She never played with dolls, but by the age of eleven, she made doll clothes for her sisters' dolls. Ann admits she was never a good student in her years in the public school system. She spent class time doodling in her notebooks and around the holes punched in three-ring binder paper. All of these things helped prepare her for her career as a quilter!

Quilting since 1978, she has been passionate about designing and making her own quilts. She loves entering competitions, teaching, lecturing, and writing about quilting. Her work is always colorful with heavy thread use, and her subjects are based on her life experiences. You will find flowers, leaves, trees, water, and her cat Oreo as favorite images in her work. Professional quilters need to have a hobby, so after many years of sewing and quilting she started gardening and, like her grandmother, is serious about writing her family history.

Ann's website: www.annfahl.com

Resources

Bendable Bright Light
www.bendablebrightlight.com

Cherrywood Fabrics
www.cherrywoodfabrics.com

Fairfield Batting
www.poly-fil.com

Gingher Scissors
www.gingher.com

Hobbs Batting
www.hobbsbondedfibers.com

Janome
www.janome.com

Quilter's Vinyl
www.ctpub.com

Rowenta Irons and Steamers
www.rowentausa.com

Schmetz Sewing Machine Needles
www.schmetz.com

Sewers Aid by Collins
www.dritz.com/brands/

SewSlip
www.sewslip.com

Superior Threads
www.superiorthreads.com

Wonder-Under Paper-Backed Fusible Web
www.shoppellon.com

Also by Ann Fahl

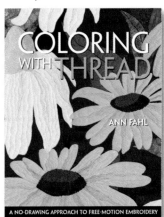

Great Titles *from* C&T PUBLISHING

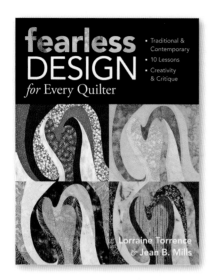

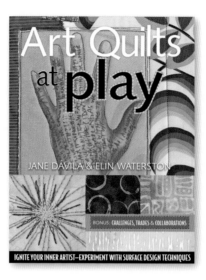

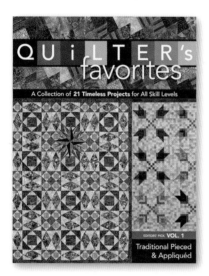

Available at your local retailer or **www.ctpub.com** *or* **800-284-1114**

For a list of other fine books from C&T Publishing, ask for a free catalog:

C&T PUBLISHING, INC.
P.O. Box 1456
Lafayette, CA 94549
800-284-1114

Email: ctinfo@ctpub.com
Website: www.ctpub.com

C&T Publishing's professional photography services are now available to the public. Visit us at www.ctmediaservices.com.

Tips and Techniques can be found at www.ctpub.com > Consumer Resources > Quiltmaking Basics: Tips & Techniques for Quiltmaking & More

For quilting supplies:

COTTON PATCH
1025 Brown Ave.
Lafayette, CA 94549
Store: 925-284-1177
Mail order: 925-283-7883

Email: CottonPa@aol.com
Website: www.quiltusa.com

Note: Fabrics used in the quilts shown may not be currently available, as fabric manufacturers keep most fabrics in print for only a short time.